The Long Run

Meditations on Marriage, Dementia, Caregiving, and Loss

Richard J. Sherry

St. Paul, Minnesota

Contents

Introduction: Writing this book

I have started this book in my imagination dozens of times. I think I know why: I am trying to share with others what it has been like to love another person, and to watch her grow and mature from our teenage years, and then fade and wither under dementia, until her death almost 12 years after diagnosis. Questions about how to start, how to structure this story, what distance to maintain, how revealing, how vulnerable—all of them rattle around, shouting at me, demanding I take a position and stick to it.

It's not like I don't have enough material, as I've been walking through the last ten years. I have letters, medical reports, photos, my wife's journals (increasingly fragmented), her prayers, her meditations, thinning down and narrowing until they are mechanical repetitions of the day's activities, and then ceasing altogether. I have essays I've written.

How do you tell the story of a long love, half a century holding hands? We were Candice Elaine Shearer and Richard James Sherry, and for half a century we were Rich and Candy.

When I've thought about this narrative in the past, day by day, I've often thought of it in terms of Don Henley and Glenn Frey singing "The Long Run."

Who can go the distance?
We'll find out in the long run.
We can handle some resistance
If our love is a strong one.[1]

All of us in deep relationships want to believe that "we can handle some resistance." We want to make that long run. But in the real-world marriage has an end, and the traditional marriage vows insist that we face it. Look at the marriage vows like those Candy and I repeated—which contain both an affirmation from the bride and groom *to the pastor* and an affirmation *to the community and to one another.*

> The Pastor asks the groom:
> P: _Name_____, will you have this woman to be your wife, to live with her in holy marriage according to the Word of God? Will you *love her, comfort her, honor her, and keep her in sickness and in health and, forsaking all others, be husband to her as long as you both shall live?*
> A: I Will

"Until death parts us." Mutual unreserved commitment, shared unstinting performance, right up to the end: the long run. Four days before she died, on our anniversary, our son Peter posted a picture of us walking down the aisle, moments married, with poetry from William Blake and a thank-you: *"Thanks for showing up for each other, over and over again."*

Whether we regard our vows as promises to be kept or an ideal we need to strive to achieve, it's still out there: "until death parts us." It's part of every religious tradition. Even do-it-

---

[1] Henley, Don, and Glenn Frey (1979). "The Long Run." On *The Long Run.* Asylum Records.

yourself vows have things like, I promise "to love you and be by your side through all the days and nights of our lives."

An author I've read notes that one of the "Basic Rules of Flying" is that "The air has edges." We casually think of flying as unlimited three-dimensional movement in space, but the air has edges, the ground and space, both where you run out of air to support you. Our vows in marriage acknowledge one edge: when death parts us. And somehow, we need to find a way to go on in light of that edge, both before we reach it and after.

So, here's my focus. This is not a book about "marriage" in general. It is not a book of recommendations on "how to do it." It is my story about a part of our marriage, the last part, how from 2006 to 2018—and especially these last years—Candy moved toward death, and I tried to care for her and ease that going. And it is about what comes after. In this story, I am not heroic, nor is she, and death is not a villain. Neither are we victims. We are Christians, and we ask the same questions everyone asks. We are changed by these experiences. This is about the long run and the edge.

And this is not a book about answers, except in rare places. It is a way of looking at what partners are likely to encounter, as we stumbled into them.

Along the way, I've dated many of the meditations. Some of them are "real time," with dates from when I posted about our lives on Facebook. They are the closest to the personal experience of those days. Others are larger in scope, addressing themes in marriage and caregiving.

Chapter 1

January 27, 2018: How We Ended

On that Saturday, a bright, clear winter day in St. Paul, my wife Candy stopped breathing. Kathryn, a friend who was reading a Psalm to her, said her breathing slowed, and slowed, and stopped as she finished reading. She was turned on her side, looking at white flowers sent by students from many years ago, and at the blue sky beyond them out the north window.

I was on an errand, and Kathryn called me in the car. She said, "You should come home now." I asked, "Is Candy all right?" And Kathryn said, "She's just stopped breathing." I turned the car around and was home 20 minutes later. I came around the bed, where her eyes were still open, looking out the window, kissed her on the forehead, and gently laid my cheek against hers. She was still warm. And I said good-bye.

That morning, I had given her a dropper of water between her cheek and her gum, and gently cleaned her teeth and mouth, and held her, bending over her on her hospital bed in our second bedroom. She seemed unchanged over the last two days, withdrawn into herself, silent as she had been for the last three years, struggling a little with breathing, hands curled and more rigid. She had been unable to eat without choking for two days. She was frail, that long lovely body, now a hundred pounds lighter. I had changed her brief, tended the sores on her bottom and tailbone where her skin was breaking down, and tried to find a position with pillows that would ease her breathing and not put pressure on the wounds.

And now all that was done. We had been married 47 years and 4 days, and in love half a century. She was 68 years old, and had been headed for this end for the last eleven years.

Chapter 2

Winter 1971 - 2000: Where We Started

Candy and I were married on a cold, almost-snowy Saturday in January, 1971. First semester finals had ended, Candy had graduated, I had another semester to go, and we had a week for a honeymoon. We had started dating in our freshman year, the fall of 1967, gotten engaged in the summer of 1969, and now were starting life together. I loved this tall, slender, shy, happy brunette—as tall as I was, as shy as I was, witty, quiet, bright. We were both very young Christians, if you date that from when one makes a serious and reasoned commitment to try to live faithfully to Christ's teaching.

We were, in January 1971, laughably ignorant. No, we didn't know what we were getting into, and we stepped into marriage a hundred miles away from both sets of parents, trying to finish college (me) and start graduate school (Candy), earn enough money to live on, and discover how actually to love and please each other. We had no training in how to fight fair, how to work together, how to negotiate differences in family culture, and on and on. We talked a lot about the future, and dreams we had—I was set on teaching English at the college level, and I've never wavered from that—but the further I got away from that central desire, the fuzzier I was. Like a lot of new couples, we were (as I remember) pretty inept at everything else. We could balance our checkbooks, and that was about it. Like everyone, we were discovering that sexual attraction didn't mean that we actually knew how to build an enduring relationship.

The one thing we had going for us was our church home, which included friends who loved us and (we thought) which included more mature believers who could give us a clue. That small church, and the friends we had—many of whom were excited for us—continued to be our "family" that first semester.

I was waiting for graduate school acceptances, and information on financial aid. Washington State, where we were, had already accepted me, as had several other universities, all places my faculty advisors had recommended. But nobody was offering financial aid at that point, and I had no idea how to earn enough money for tuition, let alone enough to live on. And then suddenly the University of Illinois came through with an acceptance and aid enough that we thought we could make it—including a tuition waiver as long as I was a teaching assistant. We took it in a heartbeat.

And then we were faced with a summer—or most of it— with little or no income, followed by what would almost certainly be a U-Haul move across half the country. Out of nowhere came a suggestion that we get involved with the university's Victorian melodrama production, the Summer Palace, which wouldn't pay much if anything but would get us supper every day and friends to hang out with. And, because God does in fact often protect innocents, we signed up. Candy and I set up and ran the box office, I learned how to hang lights and run the lighting board, and we turned six weeks of waiting into friendships. And we were still learning how to love each other and talk together.

When the Palace season ended, we packed the car with everything we had and spent a week with Candy's folks in Spokane. They made the gracious offer that they'd go with us as far as Iowa, because they had family there and it'd be fun to tent-camp for several nights across the country. Dave (Candy's brother) talked her folks into putting the boat trailer behind the Malibu, and so, Falcon-with-U-Haul, Malibu-with-ski-boat, we crossed the Rockies in Idaho, through Montana and Wyoming, and ended in Northwest Iowa. I think they quite sensibly wanted to make sure that Candy arrived safely at least as far as they could go. And so we arrived in Champaign-Urbana, Illinois, in late August, 1971, trying to get settled into a basement studio apartment a few blocks from campus and discover this new town.

Within a couple of days, we made contact with the small Lutheran church where we'd spend our first three years. The young guy who greeted us as we walked in on a midweek afternoon was the brand-new pastor, Gene Peisker, who had, with wife Jan and a small troop of boys, just transferred from Eastern Montana. They were exactly who we needed to meet: cheerful despite a big move, deeply spiritual, as shy in some ways as we were, and like us, trying to understand the Midwest.

And then, right at the start of registration at the university, we met others in a religious organization which became our "fellowship." And they didn't immediately know what to do with us. They hadn't a clue what do to with married graduate students. Two weeks later, we got an invitation to join another couple and be part of a Bible study. Now, we'd been churchgoers for a long, long time, but I was relatively new as someone who really had decided that this "Christian" thing was real, and that I needed it. And churchgoing Candy knew her Bible, and thought she could manage this.

What we found, with Roger and Soni Glick, was an introductory Bible study in the Gospel of John that focused on how people first met Jesus. We felt—even with the strangeness of new relationships, new town, and on and on—that these folks could be friends. And they were, for several years, until new adventures moved them on. Through them, we met others, and found ourselves in a community.

A word about these last three paragraphs: I mention them because they were essential support structures for us, as they are for many young couples. They provided models for us of how to live together, as well as what seemed like a coherent world and life view. They provided friends, when we were a thousand miles from where we'd grown up. Whether you, reader, come from a faith tradition or none at all, friends and community likely play an important role in shaping who you are. These were ours.

I'm skipping ahead a lot here: two graduate degrees, job interviews, a newborn son, a first academic job—that lasted seventeen years—a newborn daughter, a graduate degree for Candy, first work outside the home that led to a career, travel in the summers, and then a second job in Minnesota hundreds of miles away from our settled lives in Kentucky. Those newborns were in high school and one in college.

Candy's health became problematic in the middle of all this, with a heart condition that appeared when she was 35 and led to medication, implanted defibrillators—three, by the end—and changes in our lives. And then—small at the time, momentous in retrospect—an evening meal in 2000, sitting together with our daughter Emily, at home in Minnesota.

"Dad, why do you always finish Mom's sentences?" she asked. The question did not feel as intimidating as it sounds. Candy looked up at Em across the dinner table, and said something like, "Because if I can't find the word, he knows what I want to say."

Chapter 3

Summer, 2006: Diagnosis

Candy was diagnosed with Primary Progressive Aphasia (PPA) in the summer of 2006. We knew that something was wrong, that she was losing words and struggling with reading and speaking, and got a referral to a neurologist in our healthcare organization. The neurologist reviewed findings from a speech and language therapist Candy had visited. When we met with her, she gave Candy a brief examination as we sat together and then told us what she thought might be happening.

No, I think I remember her saying in response to our questions, *it's likely not Alzheimer's. It's almost certainly not a stroke, because it's progressive, and it's been slow. What you likely have is something called Primary Progressive Aphasia. There's never been any medication for this, and as far as we know, there's no cure.* And then she added, *It's not fatal, but somewhere along the way, it will affect memory and judgment and develop into dementia. It will affect the emotions and central brain functions like appetite and movement. At some point, it might affect her ability to swallow, to eat, and she might choke. And that*, I think she said, *does mean it will kill you.*

What she recommended was some coping strategies, including visits to a psychologist and language therapist. *But not soon,* I thought. *Thank God, it will not kill her soon.* I don't think Candy really understood the implications of that diagnosis, but we knew things would have to change. I think we agreed that we would, though, try to keep on going as long as we could. At the time she was working as a reference librarian at a local private college, driving herself to work and home daily, and I was working at a different private college two miles further north in the Twin Cities. We kept going, and I realize now that I was compartmentalizing a lot of this in order to keep functioning at work and at home. Compartments leak. When I was invited to offer prayer for the congregation in church a couple of weeks after the diagnosis, I found myself standing at the lectern almost unable to finish, overcome with emotion that no one else seemed to sense.

Chapter 4

2007 and Early 2008: Confirmation

We had follow up visits with the neurologist, and in late 2007, with the speech and language therapist and psychologist the doctor had recommended. The results of the testing quantified, in some measure, how much she had lost, and in what areas of language and thinking. The neurologist we'd seen initially referred us to the Mayo Clinic in downstate Minnesota, two hours away.

In February, 2008, I drove us down for a day, followed up with another visit several days later. After a PET scan, which showed some significant brain tissue atrophy, Candy sat with a speech pathologist while I watched from another chair. The doctor's report rehearses what was for me about thirty minutes of hair-stand-on-end shock.

Verbal expression: Mrs. Sherry had severe difficulty with confrontation naming, naming only 7 of the first 20 items on the Boston Naming Test. At that point, the test was discontinued due to the significant amount of time it took her for each response and due to her frustration. Examples of her error responses are as follows: For flower, she replied "something growing outside;" for helicopter, she replied, "airport;" for broom, she replied "cleaning your floor;" for octopus, she replied "animal;" for "hanger," she replied, "that is what I put my clothes in." These responses indicated that for many of the items she could not name, she did know what the item was and could often tell me something about it. There were two articles which she did not even recognize. These included "whistle" and "mushroom." For these two, she could not choose the correct item even when given two or three choices, as she really did not even recognize the word. This also happened when following verbal commands where she did not even recognize the word "thumb." She was able to define 2/5 words, telling me that a bargain was a "good deal" and to repair was "to fix." She could not tell me that a robin was a bird, and this was another instance of not even recognizing the word. She could not recognize the word "robin," even when she was shown a picture of one, and could not choose the word "bird" out of three choices.

Reading and writing: She was able to read and correctly answer 6/8 yes/no questions and 7/8 multiple choice questions. She was able to follow only 1 of 4 verbal directions ("touch your nose"); anything longer or more complex was too difficult for her. Oral reading was characterized by occasional word level errors. Paragraph reading was especially slow, and she had a great deal of difficulty with recall/ comprehension.

Mrs. Sherry was able to write five words to dictation without spelling error. She wrote three sentences to dictation, misspelling only "caught" and "tornado." Her self-generated paragraph is as follows; "This summer we will be going to Alaska in June. We fly to Seattle, Washington, first, then we go in the water up to Alaska. In July, my husband's brothers and their wives will be coming to Minnesota. We will all go up to Grand Marais [a small town in northeastern Minnesota] together and stay in a friend's home. It is good that I will not be working at the library any more, so our summertime activities will be good."

The primary Mayo neurologist also included that Candy had stopped watching television and movies "because she has difficulty understanding what is going on. She has substantially reduced the amount of reading that she does for pleasure because she finds that reading is much slower than it used to be. She has difficulty following conversations in social situations, particularly in large groups."

But she continued to drive, she told them, and wasn't getting lost. She continued to do most of the shopping and cooking, although she reported that "following a recipe is difficult because she will not recognize the name of an item."

I drove us home late that afternoon, up Highway 52 from Rochester, feeling as bleak and cut down as the corn stubble left in the fields. Both of us were wordless.

A week later, the senior Mayo neurologist encouraged us to try a new treatment for aphasia, on the basis of some research which showed that isolated cases responded to immunotherapy medication. One woman in particular, after large doses of prednisone had reported a significant reversal of symptoms.

In March 2008, Candy had a five-day course of intravenous methylprednisone at our local hospital, and then tapered off the dose over several weeks, taking decreasing doses orally. In reporting to the doctor later, she said that she had improved somewhat, being able to read more easily and to watch television, and found talking easier and listening much better.

As she tapered down, however, she found her symptoms retreated to the baselines, or declined further. By October, when we followed up at Mayo, while she had improved in some areas, she was worse in others. The doctors reported the results as "discouraging."

In the middle of all of this, as Candy's "narrative" to the speech pathologist had announced, she retired in late spring. She'd worked for ten years at Northwestern College, and her friends threw her a retirement party which our kids and grandchildren attended. I sat with her as her friends told her how much they appreciated her and her work. She was happy to see so many people that she'd worked with, and friends from church. What no one seemed to realize was that she didn't remember the names of many of them. She smiled and welcomed everyone.

Chapter 5

Summer 2008: Packing in Life

When I look back at 2008, a watershed year—Candy's retirement, diagnosis, therapy, and evaluation at Mayo—I'm in danger of overlooking how full that year was. In early June, we took a two-week cruise and land tour to Alaska. I'd been there in 1960 with my grandfather and my twin brother, and it was amazing to see some of the same places with grown-up eyes and a partner who could share the wonder. Outside of Skagway, we stood at a pull-out just inside the Yukon Territory border, and I tried to tell her about the landscape.

In late July, my brothers and their families joined us in Grand Marais, up near the tip of the "Arrowhead" of Minnesota, on Lake Superior. This was either the second or third "Family-Reunion-Where-No-One-Has-To-Die-First," as we called them. We had three children along as well as the four couples together, Bob and Marcia and Mike and Anne in Grand Marais and Tom and Karla and Candy and me at our friends' house east of town. It was a great week of laughter, meals together, walks on pebble beaches, and a memorable day of golf on a course where every hole overlooked the big lake. Candy and her sisters-in-law enjoyed the children, walked around town, and talked.

Later that summer, Candy drove by herself to western Minnesota to visit family for a wedding, reconnecting after more than 30 years. She planned meticulously for the weekend, drove there by herself, and checked in with me twice by phone. All seemed well when she returned, talking with me about all the people she'd seen and how they were connected.

Later that fall, Candy and I flew to Arizona, staying in a timeshare in Phoenix and visiting old friends, sightseeing, and hiking around town in the "in-the-city" mountains in the Phoenix Mountain Preserve. Despite her ongoing heart issues, she hiked with me up rough trails and we sat and enjoyed the view together. One of my favorite pictures shows her resting for a moment, looking into the distance with a smile.

In between all of these, Candy recorded the events of her days in a journal. *Voluntary cataloger for several faculty at Bethel, organizing their office libraries, and doing President Barnes' office library. Exercising at Lifetime Fitness, doing water aerobics in the morning and walking the treadmills in the evening.* Highlighting cakes, cookies, special breads, holiday treats prepared over months.

But her language skills are failing, even as you read the journal, and I don't know how to decide whether it's more than that—that is, that her cognitive skills might have been declining at the same time. So much of how we gauge intelligence is based in language and expression. She describes her water aerobics class as "water games." On Thanksgiving she wrote, *"Arranged to spend givings. We went to LTF* [LifeTime Fitness]. *Big supper work for Thanksgiving with Pete and Nichool* [Nicole] *(Eliot and Taylor) and desert also with Emily and Scot (Micah)."* It's not just spelling.

When I look at her "activity" journal, which she kept for the next four years, I don't know what to make of it. She records the daily tasks, like lots of laundry; where we went to eat, if not at home; household chores; times I traveled, or times we traveled together. With every page, fewer and fewer details are included.

Chapter 6

March 2010: Warning Signs

In March 2010, for the first time, she got lost in town while driving. She could not find a women's health facility for a checkup and so came home. I had to drive her there two days later. I didn't think a lot of it, as this was an annual visit in an area of town she seldom visited, and we were pre-GPS.

But her "activities journal" doesn't mention an accident in the car in 2009 that meant it spent two weeks in the body shop. She doesn't mention that late in 2010 she lost her driver's license, and so shifted to walking around the neighborhood during the day.

Perhaps the most noticeable feature of the journal is that she records nothing of her emotions, or reflections, or what she thought about any of the events, or family, or anything. It's as though there's no analysis, no perspective, no larger picture. On New Year's Day, 2011, she wrote, *"Fixed house by changing things Rich had done last month back to normal."* That's her description of putting away the Christmas decorations and tree, an event that used to be a highlight, full of laughter and memories of the ornaments we'd collected.

The journal ends, winding down, in September 2012. By that time, she was recording only the year and the day, not even the date, having lost track of the month several times during the previous six months.

Candy also kept a private journal reflecting on her spiritual life. Daily, she'd list passages she read in the Bible, with perhaps a page of comment or a prayer written out. In her spiritual journal, she is deeply troubled, fatigued, without energy. After a visit in February 2010 to her neurologist she wrote, addressing God directly, "*I was almost feeling like ending my life after being with her—I was very tired—so my nap and now time with you is so important.*" A week later, she prays, "*Can I follow You rather than just my big list of 'does'?!*" A few days later, "*Lord, with my reading problems may I still be connected with You!*"

Over February, March, and April 2010, her journals show her frustration with words, her desire to "connect" with God and with others, her attempts to accomplish things around the house and at work. By May, as she's decided to retire from any work outside the home, even cataloguing, many of her journal entries recount how she feels "useless," "overwhelmed." But she celebrates her first day as a "full-time home maker!" on June 2nd, wanting to do more reading, and it's clear she feels less pressure with responsibilities.

Chapter 7

Losing an Anchor

Families, no matter how different, have some commonalities. One of them, despite changes in gender roles over time, is that parents often are anchors. They're sources of wisdom, knowledge passed down, understanding processes, and the wall we bounce our thoughts and hopes against.

Sometimes, our "anchors" pass on or are the keepers of family lore. When her mother died in 2004, Candy inherited the "Book of Remembrance" her mother had developed—the Shearer and Kroeger family tree and all its branches, with photos of cousins long gone, tracing the family in Iowa and South Dakota. She inherited Eunice's recipes, family favorites for generations, things we still make in our separate households.

We began to lose this wisdom in 2010. I saw it firsthand, but Peter and Emily saw it too. Peter recently wrote me his impressions of episodes in 2009 and later.

Perhaps the first signs I saw of mom's decline were when she started to use key "anchor phrases" over and over, such as "steps of possibilities," which was one that I heard a lot when I would talk with her about how things were going during my divorce and then my second marriage.

One particular moment that stood out to me that made me realize she didn't quite understand what was being said to her was when I started graduate school to become a marriage and family therapist, instead of returning to seminary to finish my MDiv. She was attempting to be encouraging about school as I left one day, and said "I hope everyone has a special time with the Lord today." Part of me wanted to correct her, as theological study wasn't my aim anymore, but I didn't. For her, any time was a potential special time with the Lord.

But the moment that really solidified that sense that something wasn't right anymore was when I brought dinner over for her once when dad was out of town for work. He had suggested pizza, but I decided to change things up with fried chicken - something I'd seen mom eat a hundred times, if once. I wasn't eating with her, as I had already had dinner, and as she raised the drumstick to her mouth and tried to bite into the thinner, bony end, I realized that she didn't recognize it as chicken, and didn't know how to eat it as she once had. From then on, I began to watch for the other signs of dementia that inevitably came.

I felt especially lost during these times [in 2014-2015], *as my second marriage was failing harder and faster than my first, and I didn't have mom's strong but gentle wisdom to guide me.*

I also shared his sense of loss. An anchor stabilizes you at night, or when the wind or tide are moving your craft around. You sleep easier, even in harbor. More and more, like Peter I was struggling to respond to events as they happened.

Chapter 8

Wandering

One of the things that terrifies caregivers is "wandering," when your partner, confused, "gets away," outside the home or suddenly "out of contact." As I think about this, more episodes than I want to remember are out there.

The first episode was at our timeshare in Orlando, one evening in 2011. It was our first night there, and we were—as everyone is—tired after travel and a little disoriented. Our one-bedroom ground-floor apartment had a bathroom with a door into the bedroom and another door into the hall toward the living room. Candy awoke in the night, went to the bathroom, and went out the hall door, out the front door (which locked behind her), and walked into the humid night, down the front of the apartment block in her (admittedly modest) nightgown. For some reason one apartment was unlocked, and she walked in, found a bedroom, and lay down.

I awoke a few minutes later, could not find her, called security, pulled on clothes, and walked outside, key in hand. A few minutes later, a security officer pulled up, called my name, and led me to the apartment where she'd been found. The family designated to stay there had just arrived, found her in the bed, and called security just about the time I did. She likely wasn't gone from the apartment for more than a few minutes. When we went back, I put a chair in front of the door and did so every night afterward. The possibilities for harm in situations like this are enormous, of course. Within a day Candy'd forgotten the whole thing, as if it were a bad dream. I was shaken.

A year or so later, back in Minnesota, visiting friends outside Grand Marais, she went for a walk she'd taken forty or fifty times, down a road below the cabin. Out the back yard, down a path through grass and bushes, and onto the road. We'd always done a simple "out and back," a stretch of road little traveled, a "siding" off the main highway but connecting to it at both ends, a mile and a half long. When she didn't return as planned, I got in the car, pulled out of the driveway, and saw her walking on the main highway a quarter mile away. I picked her up a moment later, and she explained that she'd forgotten where she was supposed to turn. We went to church, where I prayed fervently to be smarter next time.

One autumn afternoon when we were home in the Twin Cities, I couldn't raise her on the phone when I called from the office. I drove home immediately, realized she was gone from the house—wearing her pink parka—and called the local sheriff's office. Ten minutes later a deputy delivered her to the front door. She'd walked into the nature center across the way, missed a turn on a path, and walked out the other side. The "other side" was a hundred yards from the sheriff's substation, and the deputy who brought her home had just pulled out of the parking lot when—there she was!—on the sidewalk.

One I didn't even know about. She went walking away from the house, turned at the end of the block, and instead of doing an "out and back" ended up making a loop over four miles long on a chilly autumn day. She explained when I got home that she'd gone on a longer walk than she'd planned, and left it at that. When I sat down with her at supper, I slowly got the details from her. I remember holding my breath for a second as she finished, in part because it seemed like her sense of threat or danger was entirely absent.

For two years, every week Candy walked a quarter-mile to the elementary school near us and reshelved books for the school librarian, who was perpetually overworked. I got a call at work from the librarian one day near noon, asking if Candy had gotten home safely. She'd been alarmed, she said, when she realized that Candy was walking on a busy street—if only a quarter-mile—because she perceived her as "unsafe" out there. We talked further, and the librarian agreed to tell her that she didn't need to come in any more. I knew she was at home, because we'd talked on the phone, but I appreciated the librarian's concern. Candy, on the other hand, was a little frustrated with the decision.

"Wandering" has become a common-enough phenomenon that you often see family members appealing for help on Facebook. "So and so has disappeared from her home." We have "silver alerts," telling us that a senior has driven away in his or her car, and hasn't reported in. We are caught in powerful emotions here: do we empower or aid our loved ones by giving them freedom, or do we put them in the care of professionals who must, with the best will in the world, imprison them?

The year before I retired, I contacted a local office of the national company "HomeInstead Senior Care," and arranged for a woman to meet Candy at the house and walk with her for an hour. In bad weather, they went to a local mall and walked a mile together. She enjoyed her "companions," and they delivered her home, made sure she was secure, and then called me to debrief.

She didn't resent the companionship and seemed to understand that these women were there to help and to talk with her. I knew she was safe with them, and that they understood her limitations. In the end, I made sure she never left the house alone. As she became more confused and uncertain, having me with her gave her more security, and when we walked, we held hands like teenagers again.

Chapter 9

On Saying What Needs to Be Said

The next chapter is going to be about "intimacy." So is this, in a way. It's about "keeping short accounts," as friends used to describe it. "Don't let the sun go down on your anger," we used to hear, as many married couples have heard from parents. It's true: it's a good idea to keep short accounts, and pay the bill in full—an apology, a request for forgiveness, an admission of a mistake or a hurtful word. Sometimes, it's listening to understand how you have injured someone. At some point in dementia, the words you want to say will be unheard, or not understood.

In "New Kid in Town," the Eagles lament, "There's so many things you should have told her." Even when you're as open as you can be, you feel this way when your partner is struggling to understand. You want to share your love, your tears, your fears, your hopes, and what you are left with in aphasia is the resolution to be kind, and thoughtful, and present, and patient, because behavior is what matters now, not words.

Peter wrote me recently about an experience in late 2017.

One of my last experiences with mom was when I visited her alone in a nursing home while she was getting some respite care. I had written her a letter, and I shared some things with her that I hadn't ever told her before. The mind is ultimately a great mystery, and I don't know how much or how little she cognitively received during that time, but I did have a sense that a certain sense of peace had fallen on the room and between us, and I told her as I left that even if she would not remember that moment, I would carry it for both of us.

And sometimes, that's what we're left with, the hope that someone understands. Say what needs to be said, then, early and often. There will be a time when words fail.

Chapter 10

Spring 2015: Intimacies

Two of my three half-sisters (all Massachusetts women, all older than I by a few years) I think would understand the language I will use. They are widows, one fairly recently. When Sally lost Walter, it was after years of diabetes and its complications, and the hurt of seeing a vigorous, decent, bright, delightful man worn down. I am sorry not to have known him better, and frankly glad that we lived far enough away that I did not see what must have been extraordinarily painful for both of them.

One of the most challenging parts of Candy's path of dementia was the loss of intimacy. I don't mean sex, although of course I mean sex, as part of it. I mean over and above all that the sense of profound partnership that began shortly after we first laced our hands together and went walking on an October night in Pullman, half a century ago.

Intimacy is this sense of shared history, of dreams, of longings, of understanding the present and shaping the future in our conversations. There were times in college where we just talked about the kind of world we wanted to shape together, the kind of home, and where, and how we wanted to live. At night, after we were married, we would lay in bed together, and spin dreams—when I got The Degree, and when I got The Job, and Where We Would Go, and children's names and all of that. It is like Dr. Seuss telling us about the places we'll go. It is in the words in our throats, and the breath in our lungs.

Intimacy is the sitting together, my arm over her shoulder, and her curled against me, talking quietly, or simply watching the world together. It is the long—I mean really long rides in the car, from Kentucky to Minnesota, or Connecticut, or California, or Spokane. When you spend two or three days with one another, especially before air conditioning, you are sorting out, all the time, the physical space and how you will be together on a summer drive between South Dakota cornfields. It is admiring the way the Absaroka Range looms up next to you all the way to Big Timber, Montana, or that shared surprise as you dip down into Livingston. It is a pot of green tea with cherry together on a frosty Minnesota evening. It is "collaborative" double solitaire, lying across the bed, before we turn the lights out. It is in the gestures and the touch and the caress and the tenderness.

It is about how you are together not just intellectually, but also, because we were religious people, spiritually. Candy was raised in a fairly traditional and conventional Lutheran home, where her dad led the household—but where her mom was the deeper, more conventionally consistent Christian. Roy faced the world (that traditional image of masculinity for a century, especially in the rural West), and Eunice faced inward, caring for the family. Candy really "woke up" in the faith before me, the depressed and angry and confused semi-pagan, when we were in college, so that I found her more open and more thoughtful about faith issues (and more knowledgeable —gotta love those Lutherans!) than I was. Intimacy involved recurrent and challenging discussions about how what we believed played out in daily life, about obedience, about following. As often as I did, she took the counter-cultural position, and I learned from her as much as she learned from me. Intimacy is about the posture of humility and about the direct glance of thankfulness and affirmation.

Intimacy is in this profound trust we experience when we yield our bodies and our hopes and our futures and our present to this other person, and when we receive from him or her that selfsame gift. It is "exchange," in the sense the English author Charles Williams and others meant it, the free gift offered between equals who value and respect this one other person as much as they do themselves.

Intimacy is that bedrock of history over which the stream of the daily flows. There is that streambed, when all else is gone.

In the course of this walk downhill, this shallow path, this daily descent, all these things were being lost every minute. Words, gestures, touch, that sense of a shared look at the world around us, any semblance of exchange—all these are redefined over weeks and months. You are walking on a road, and then a trail, and then a path, and then a tightrope. Something out there is peeling away the warmth and support in your life, that stabilizing hand you held, that voice of balance that kept you from panic or giddiness, folly or fear. I mean that for Candy, losing the connections of memory, and also for me.

Susan Sarandon in *Shall We Dance?* tells Richard Jenkins' character, the private detective Devine, that people get married "Because we need a witness to our lives." I never saw this movie when Candy was alive, but the deep, shocking truth of that statement is undeniable. You say to your partner, Sarandon's Beverly says, "Your life will not go unnoticed, because I will notice it. Your life will not go unwitnessed, because I will be your witness."

And in the middle of losses like these, you begin to suspect that you will be stripped back to holding memories only. Dante says of the souls in Limbo that they are "spared the fire / And suffering Hell in one affliction only: / That without hope we live on in desire."

I do not think I ever lost hope, but I know I was clinging to rags and tatters of it. Every day, I had the sense of something sifted out, lost. My witness was fading, and how do you measure your earthly life without that? And how must it have felt to her, to lose those shared histories, even the recognition of the faces of those we loved?

Candy knew it as well as I; even though she lost words week by week, and memories, until there seemed almost nothing left, when we lay together in bed, she tucked herself against me, underneath my arm, and would slip into sleep. We were a long way from "first love," even from sexual romance, but "comfort" and "home" remained.

In April 2015 an early morning experience with her led me to write this.

Early Saturday morning, after midnight,
You awoke, and I could not quiet you.
You threw the covers off, and edged out of bed,
Lit only by the nightlight from the bath beyond.
I called, "Candy, come back to bed. No one
Is in the other room. I'm here. Come."
I closed my eyes, listening, seeing in my mind
Your hand on the bedpost by my feet, paused,
Considering.
Who knows what is in your mind these days,
As the neurons flicker, weaker, tangled, hesitant?
I opened my eyes.
You stood above me, looking down in the dark,
Your face inches away, wide-eyes, lips parted in a smile.
And you leaned down and touched your lips to mine,
Remembering, I hope, a half century of intimacy, of care.
"Kiss me again and again, for your love is sweeter than wine."
"Give me a thousand kisses, then a hundred.
Let us shake the abacus, so that no one may know the number."

Wordless, smiling, you bent again, and kissed me,
And came to bed, nestling under my arm, and I thought,
"It is enough. For this moment, it is enough."

Chapter 11

Concealment

I've mentioned that at Candy's retirement party she almost certainly didn't remember the names of people she'd worked with. Over the years of her illness, she lost more and more of her memories, both short and long term. And for most of that time, she successfully concealed it. And sometimes, she even did so with me.

After about 2008 or so, her memory became unreliable. In her work as a reference librarian, she helped college students negotiate finding information—sources for papers, specific tools to help them, guidance in how to narrow a research question. We talked about it in the evening after work, and she shared how one day she couldn't remember the names of the tools to use. But she'd found a workaround, she thought: ask the student questions, and lead them to the tools that would provide answers. She was right, and she was able to work for another year before retiring.

Some of the work she did in the technical services area, such as cataloging, depended less on knowledge of specific facts and more on process knowledge. She had a routine established for how to handle a new book that had arrived, and software to assist her in assigning a call number. Although I didn't realize it, she'd made a "process" list for many of these tasks so that she could follow through with them. Her work continued, although at a slower pace. Sometimes, she brought work home for her home computer, although I didn't realize it.

I also didn't realize that she was practicing a kind of "cover-up" of her abilities in other areas. Instead of doing her usual grocery shopping during the week, we'd go together on Saturday mornings, working through her list and a handy map of the shelves that the store provided. Meals got simpler, although I didn't catch on. Over a couple of years, she stopped baking, without letting on that the recipes were too complicated, and depended on judgment that she couldn't manage. A whole set of workarounds to conceal lost abilities, and I never caught on.

One evening after she'd retired we had our regular evening at the local gym. After an hour's exercise, I asked her to wait in the entryway while I brought the car up to the portico. It'd been raining and cold, and we were parked halfway down the lot. By the time I pulled up at the entry, she wasn't there. I got out and walked toward the door. As I glanced back at the car standing ahead of me, I realized that she'd gotten into someone else's car, and the driver was trying to convince her she'd made a mistake. I knocked on the window, her face burst into a smile, and she climbed out. "I thought it didn't look right," she said, and laughed it off. We got home safely, but I resolved not to leave her alone when we were out.

I know I was complicit in this, to some extent. In January, 2011, we took a long weekend and flew back to our hometown, Spokane, to visit family and to attend Christ Lutheran Church, where we'd been married 40 years to the day before. On Friday, we visited a couple who had been her parents' friends, and before you knew it we were called out in the Sunday worship service—"stand up, stand up!"—and invited to a cake and punch reception after the service. *So much for low profile*, I thought. Many parishioners came up to greet us—and especially Candy, whose parents had been active, long-term members. And neither of us knew most of them—and Candy, perhaps, none. I am not sure, now, that she even knew why we were there.

Process knowledge of ordinary things began to evaporate. Even before she retired, I noticed that she was having difficulty with her makeup. Of course, I knew nothing about makeup, but I could tell that she wasn't blending her foundation makeup down below her jawline, so the makeup stopped abruptly at the jaw line, making her look like she was wearing a mask. Whenever I saw it, I'd call it to her attention, and she'd dutifully step into the bathroom and fix it. I didn't connect it to memory loss, not for a long time.

Something similar—loss of process knowledge—happened more frequently later. Difficulties running a software program she'd used for years. Frustration because Microsoft Solitaire wouldn't let her play the way she wanted to. Forgetting how to use the telephone.

Only afterwards have I begun to see how Candy was trying to manage "normal" when things were crumbling. I suspect that this is actually more common than we know. One of my brothers calls this "normalcy bias." "We expect people to do things a certain way and to a certain level because we have seen them always do so. We cannot understand, and often do not recognize, when they do not do things the way we expect," he commented. If I hadn't sat in during her Mayo Clinic interviews, or even the first meeting with our local neurologist, I wouldn't have recognized what she was really facing. The more memory slips away, the thinner the ice you're walking on. And perhaps, the harder you work to conceal what is gone.

She may not even have recognized how much she had lost, although her journals hint at it. But all this time she was adapting to try to maintain life as she knew it.

I think she was determined not to let me know, for a long time. I don't believe she was afraid I'd leave her, or anything like that, but perhaps that I'd think less of her, even that she wasn't "holding her end up" somehow. Always a private person, she didn't want others to look at her as somehow failing. From the time she was in high school, I think she faced what we call now the "impostor syndrome," feeling that we're not as good as others think we are. Candy was high school co-valedictorian in our Spokane Valley school, but shared with me much later that she felt that her education in a small town in South Dakota—and her grades—were not the same quality as our Spokane school. Even though she was a National Merit Semifinalist—in the top half of one percent of all high schoolers—she always was slightly embarrassed to have been up there on stage. A few months before she died, our high school class had their 50th reunion, which we couldn't attend. Reflections on high school came into sharp focus for me on a day in September 2017.

We had had our first visit from a "music therapist," Molly, who played very well on guitar and sang hymns and choruses with a soprano so sweet and smooth it lifted your heart. She sat in front of Candy—we had talked about what Candy might like—and sang to her, and she smiled. Her focus on Molly, as she sat in her lift chair, was intense. I can't think why I had waited so long. Molly and I had laughed together the day before on the phone, when she mentioned she played flute as well as guitar for hospice patients. I suggested the guitar this time, but told Molly how Candy loved the flute, though she'd never played. A half a century ago, on her birthday in June, at the Central Valley commencement she and my friend Sandy Davis had been co-valedictorians. Her brief message--not as defensive as the title sounds— was "It's All Right to Play the Flute." She meant by the title that it's all right to play a beautiful thing, something different, and hard, that engages all of you, that you play with your whole body, and maybe that your parents can't see the use of. I had little or no understanding of how complicated her emotions were about her family, how uncertain she was of herself, and how she longed to be affirmed and valued, and how she often thought of herself as inadequate, unsuccessful.

Later that same September day we got a thoughtful, supportive note from a student, Connie, whom we'd known where we'd worked in Kentucky. That college's tradition was for a couple to be "advisors" to an entire entering class of students, 200 men and women from everywhere coming to a small town. Our student, now in her forties, had dropped her daughter off at the same college and was remembering. It was a thank-you note, and one assuring us of her prayers, remembering those four years we tried to be there for that class of 200 as they grew up. Before I went out to get the mail, I'd been doing that Dangerous Thing of looking at one of Candy's notebooks--as it happened, for fall semester 1985. At thirty years distance, you discover for the first time how hard those years were for Candy, so that she despaired of being the kind of model she thought those students needed. And you realize that while she was sensitive to all the hurts I was carrying—my dad was at that moment in 1985 on life support and two weeks later died, fifteen hundred miles away, that month—I was oblivious to how wounded she was.

When you find that the person you love beyond words and deeds is so entangled, you—if you're a guy—just want to put those pieces together. Sometimes, maybe never, really, you can. Connie's note was a bit of grace that told me we'd done okay. But underneath that time, there are depths unsuspected, and it might have been better to have put those hurts on the table to be handled honestly and without any veneer. Hard to do, then.

Chapter 12

Real Time: Facebook—Accumulated Losses

Sunday, November 1, 2015

A friend from far away asked about Candy, and I acknowledge I haven't talked much about our situation regarding her health. I confess that it's difficult to do, as it's easy to come across as though I'm whining. There's little you can do about "tone" on a Facebook post. In 2006, Candy was diagnosed with Primary Progressive Aphasia, which is a "catch-all" description of symptoms, rather than an analysis of causes. What that means is that over time, she has lost language skills as the language centers of the brain are affected. There are a couple of variants of this, likely on the basis of what is actually happening in the brain. And there's no good way to find out what's actually happening in the brain; we did have a PET scan done, I think in 2008 or so, which showed some decreased blood flow and brain activity in the language center. Her implanted defibrillator (for her heart arrhythmia, which began in the mid 1980's) means that she can't have an MRI.

The outcomes over time suggest that she is experiencing what is classed as a "frontotemporal dementia"--that is, affecting the temporal lobe and the frontal lobes. Memory and reasoning are affected. And this works its way over time all along the routines and repertoires of life. Five years ago, she had to stop driving, because she had "lost" some rules of the road--like when a police car is behind you with lights flashing and siren on, you should pull over. (That was, fortunately, a minor, no-accident issue.) Two years ago, she stopped being able to crochet--she had been making hot pads and other things out of all the yarn we've had around the house. Over the course of several months, she moved from "hot pad size," squares about eight inches on a side, to "coaster size," about three inches on a side. She just forgot how to make them bigger, and then one day forgot how to do them at all. Late last fall, she stopped reading her Bible and could not write her name any longer. Six months ago, she stopped playing the piano.

About the same time, I started tying her shoes. I built a railing onto the three steps down into the garage, both so I could support her going up and so she'd have a handhold going down. Three steps. In the last two months, I'm feeding her more and more, although once she sees "how," she's able to feed herself.

Like most of us spouses in such situations, you shift into "well, it has to be done, so let's pick it up" mode, even if you've never done it before. So the whole shebang, from banking and billpaying to laundry to cooking to all the other household chores somehow gets done.

And there are things you realize that your partner does not know how to do any longer, like wash her hair, or brush her teeth, or manage toileting. Candy and I get out for walks twice a day or so, going to our local health club in the evening. I drove us out West for a week this summer, and friends invited us to stay in their cabin in Grand Marais, "Up North," for a few nights a month ago. Planning well can make most things happen.

She remains cheerful, happy to be together, and enjoys our children and grandchildren, though it is unlikely that she knows who they are. (And they've been great.) She likes being in church, and even without words knows the tune and likes being with smiling people. We enjoy a small Bible study group--later this afternoon--with people who have known us over the last five or six years and watched her with affection. The prognosis is for a continued long, slow decline. The "average" life expectancy from diagnosis is 7-8 years, the longest recorded (this was several years ago) was 17. We've had nine years so far. And they've been good years. I was able to take early retirement at 64, two years ago, and am grateful for it. It has meant we could be together as this gets more challenging. She's napping, now, and I have some Bible study discussion questions I need to finish. We're good, out here. We're managing, and trust me, there's nothing heroic about this. You just keep on. Thanks for prayers.

Chapter 13

Compassion and Friends

There are places I remember, John Lennon sings. Most of us have such places. In late 1994, well before any diagnosis, a friend from my work invited Candy and me up "for the weekend" to a cabin he and his wife and another couple owned on the north shore of Lake Superior. We traveled up with them one Friday night because, as Chet said, "It's a long way, and you might get lost." They picked us up at home about 4.30, and off we went in the late fall darkness. Up to Duluth, then take a right onto Dylan's Highway 61, which goes all the way up to Thunder Bay, Ontario. We stopped for supper at a café in Two Harbors—Miller's, perhaps? Another two hours later, under a new moon and a sky full of stars, Chet and Joyce Duck showed us their three-bedroom home, with twenty feet of living room windows a hundred feet above Lake Superior. It was three miles beyond the little harbor town of Grand Marais, with its 1350 residents about a quarter of the county's population. It's the only town in a county the size of Delaware and Rhode Island together.

They and another couple had bought and renovated it a few years before, and half the Fridays in a year after work they drove the 250 miles north and east, staying until after Sunday church and driving home. Chet was registrar at the college where I worked, Joyce a third-grade teacher in a county north of the Twin Cities. Generous and gracious, hospitable to a fault, they welcomed us again and again. The Grand Marais cabin became the site for week-long summer visits, especially after they retired. We would hike with them in the Superior National Forest, or put the canoes on the roof rack of the Forester and go to Bogus Lake, or Brule, or Sawbill, or Northern Light. Their place was utterly quiet except for the sound of wind through pines or waves on the rocks two hundred feet away.

They welcomed us, and over the years, we joined them often. We "re-learned" to canoe there, and Candy learned how to snowshoe, and both of us to cross-country ski. Every trip up we'd go to Joynes' Ben Franklin, and they'd talk with friends from a small intentional community outside of town. We'd worship together in a small community church, have Sunday turkey dinner at the East Bay Hotel, and get the obligatory one-coffee-for-the-road at the Java Moose.

We continued to visit—and even had some weekends up there alone when they couldn't come—after Candy began to fail. At first, she'd bring crocheting, or go for walks with me on the harbor streets in Grand Marais, with coffee and a cookie at the Java Moose, or a meal at the Blue Water. Eventually, we couldn't canoe any longer, because she had both forgotten how and could no longer understand my directions. A ten-minute ride on a favorite lake was our last outing, when I realized she didn't know how to balance any longer. You cannot be frantic in a canoe, but you can return to the landing with all deliberate speed, and I did. The next-to-last time we were there, in March 2015, we'd made it a five-hundred-mile-day-trip, up and back, and had coffee and pie at the Blue Water, visited with our friends the McIntires, seen the maples changing on the hill north of town, and then driven home.

Chet and Joyce came to Candy's memorial service, and waved quietly and slipped away during the reception afterwards. How like them—never intruding, but always ready with hospitality.

The very last time I was in the cabin was seven weeks after Candy's death, sitting with my laptop at Joyce's kitchen table and thinking about how to write this book. All around me were memories.

I haven't been back. Some places are so full of the past and all good memories that it is hard to imagine being there again, despite the affection of the people who remain.

*****

Chet and Joyce's hospitality enabled us to become a part of Minnesota. We were welcomed, not once but repeatedly into their home, into their church, into their lives. And that brings me to something else that has occurred to me very late in this story: food.

Celebrating our common humanity, needs, and gratitude around the table seems a rare thing these days. We have our separate households, and make separate meals, except at times of holiday when families are together. But one of the moments in which we extend practical care to one another is when we bring a family a meal. During hospice, especially when we first came back from transitional care, a number of members of our church brought food over—and our Pastor, Toni Schwabe, came frequently, perhaps weekly, with soup in quart jars, pans of lasagna, cookies for dessert. Others in church followed.

I must admit, awkwardly, to being too independent or self-conscious to ask for help. That meant that I missed out on an opportunity to be consoled and loved by others, or to be supported by them. After Candy died, and I was on my own, it seemed as though help like this just faded away quickly.

A friend commented on how ironic this is, because right at the time grief is overwhelming you, folks suddenly feel they have nothing they can do to support you. But showing up with a small meal may be actually what's needed. It's part of "remembering," and by that I mean the literal, not metaphorical, work of reincorporating someone facing loss into the family, into the neighborhood. "Re-membering" is saying again, "You're a member of our household." As my friend said, "Bring food."

*****

About the time I retired, two couples from my university invited us over for dinner. Jay and Barb Barnes and Ralph and Lyn Gustafson proposed that we meet, perhaps quarterly, for conversation and encouragement. We'd known the four of them for almost 20 years, and had always enjoyed getting together, sometimes for Bible study with another couple. We'd attended the same church for many of those years. We all had children we were concerned about, or health issues that were creeping up, or parents we'd lost or were losing. We'd talk, and eat, and pray together.

We did this with Candy at the table, struggling to follow, and as the years went on, I shifted to feeding her as she sat beside me. We all adapted and carried on. The last time we met together was in our "hospice at home" in late 2017. Candy was in her transport chair, and I fed her what little I could. The two couples brought in a casserole, and salad, and dessert, and we shared and laughed and talked and eventually prayed for one another, I think. If you ever want an example of "loving to the end," and "loving in spite of," and "respect and honor no matter what," imagine the five of us talking and sharing, and including my beloved, silent and still at the end of the table, as though fully present. The president of the university, his wife, a senior development officer and his wife, making time for two retirees with bonds of love and friendship.

*****

It is another, earlier dinner, though, that tells you the most about compassion and long-term friendship. At the end of February 2016, some friends joined us one evening. We had never been able to be together much—one couple lives in the Twin Cities, one in Colorado—but we were very close in graduate school and the early years of our marriages. They'd followed us on Facebook and through Christmas letters, so they knew what lay ahead. Even with Candy unable to converse, we had supper together and five of us talked with that depth of feeling and shared affection that comes from a long history. Candy and Sue took our firstborn sons out on walks in their strollers. Candy and Peggy had gone a thousand miles by train together for a spiritual retreat. And the six of us were together for several years with a religious organization in graduate school.

Doug, in particular, seems to bat away the normal conversational filters, and we all find ourselves responding from areas we seldom uncover. Peggy brings a refreshing directness—always has—that is deeply affirming and welcoming. They're "unexpected," these cheerful, gracious, thoughtful people. And watching Bill and Sue open up conversational avenues, including everyone, keeping us laughing and celebrating, shows how they love people and care for them. From each one of them, their spirituality just radiates joy.

A snapshot: we're talking in the living room. Candy has left the table and is sort of lying down on the couch, watching, but not really able to enter into the buzz of conversation. Her sense both of passivity and guardedness is palpable. And suddenly, with a glance at each other, Sue and Peggy are both kneeling next to her, holding her hands, and talking with her. She's singing back to them, with a questioning smile. She doesn't know these people, in all likelihood, but she senses affection and interest. It is a moment—I don't think the guys notice, but perhaps they just don't intrude—that feels like friendship and love and holiness all together.

A friend has said that one of the stumbling blocks for those wanting to visit caregivers or the grieving is the perplexity of knowing what to say. Sometimes we deal with that by saying, "I thought you'd want to be alone." Even an introvert like me knows the quiet presence of those who love you is better than their absence. The Langs and the Tells came to visit, and their affection and compassion overflowed, making a hard time more bearable. The night was full of pizza, salad, and goodness.

Chapter 14

Indignities

Any marriage has moments of embarrassment, of shock, moments never to be discussed outside the house or even outside a conversation with your spouse. We never think of these when we are dating. Some of them are reserved for those early weeks of marriage. Some go along with pregnancy ("Yes, find a rest stop! Now! I have to go!") or childbirth (I have male friends who fainted during the videos on labor and delivery). A scene in the pilot of "The Marvelous Mrs. Maisel" is like this, as the young wife waits until her husband is asleep, then gets up, puts on face cream and puts curlers in her hair, and goes back to bed. In the morning, she gets up just before the alarm, cleans her face, does her makeup and her hair, then lies down and pretends to sleep until her husband shuts the alarm off. Her husband only sees that she's always beautiful. How very 1950's. "Morning mouth" doesn't exist for him.

Things change over the decades and depend on your family of origin. Candy and I were alike in issues of modesty and body consciousness. I was raised in a family of boys in the 1950's, and female anatomy was a mystery, as were things like menstrual cycles, hormone shifts, changes in libido, and on and on. I think her experience of male anatomy (which is much less complicated!) was equally mysterious, although she had a younger brother. I have age-mate friends with entirely different perspectives and habits. A couple I know (before any of us had children) never shut the door when using the toilet. Neither one. "Privacy" and its shifting definitions define our relationships—what one keeps to himself or herself, or what a couple keep to themselves. These things change as dementia intrudes.

Toileting

Candy's aphasia had gone a long way down the road, and she was almost without words when I realized that she needed help with toileting. We were in our local Walmart when she reached inside her pants and pulled out a handful of feces and looked at me in puzzlement and shock. I reached into my pocket for a handkerchief, scooped her handful into the cloth, took her hand and walked her to the car, and then home. After laying her down on a towel on the bed and cleaning her up, I helped her get to a nap, went to the local Walgreens, and bought a package of Depends. Even remembering this event produces goosebumps. I was completely in shock.

Almost from that day onward, probably in mid-2014, she was incontinent. Before bedtime I would get her settled on the toilet, finish cleaning her up, and get her ready for sleep—help her brush her teeth, get a Depends sanitary brief on her, get her nightgown on. She was not able, I think, to understand or respond to the signals her body was sending her.

It's hard to say whether men or women caregivers have a worse time caring for their opposite-sex partners' needs. I changed my son's and daughter's diapers like a lot of fathers. But cleaning up your adult partner is an order of magnitude different, and it's not just because this is another adult. You find yourself packing a messenger bag with Depends, wipes, plastic bags, a change of pants, lotion or diaper rash cream. This adult is someone with whom you've been profoundly intimate—and at the same time, there are barriers of privacy and vulnerability you may never have crossed.

I also found myself trying to find ways to anticipate her needs—planning, for instance, rest stops with family restrooms where I could walk her into the bathroom, get her undressed and seated on the toilet, clean her when she'd finished—and if necessary, change her brief for a dry or clean one. There is nothing quite like the guilt you get when you realize that your partner—this person you've loved for decades—has been sitting in a wet brief for the last half hour.

Clothing and Grooming

Candy gained and then lost weight over the course of her illness, and as she lost language I was in the position of buying clothes for her. She needed comfortable shirts and pants, underpants (at first) and then bras. Our last experience with bras was at the Hanes Outlet store a few miles north, where (shocked attendants and all) I tried to find the right size for her, walking with her into the changing room and helping an attendant undress her to try several on. Beginning in late 2014, she could no longer dress herself.

I became responsible for dressing her, and the first thing I realized was that I had no clue about dresses, slips, or stockings. Fortunately, in our casual culture, I could dress her in slacks and comfortable button-up shirts for church. She had always worn her hair in a casual side-part, and I could manage that, and keep her bangs trimmed, but hairspray went away. So did makeup. I could not—alas!—manage jewelry, so earrings stayed in the jewelry box. In mid-July 2016, I saw her attempt to bite the diamond in her engagement ring, and realized that her hands were swollen, so that the ring needed to come off. Google showed me a way to do it without hurting her, and the rings went in her jewelry box, as well.

Eating in public

Sometime about September 2015, Candy became increasingly hesitant about feeding herself. She looked at food on her plate and seemed unable to remember what to do next. I began to feed her, and, at least early on, after a few mouthfuls she would then pick up the spoon or fork and eat on her own. More and more, though, I was feeding her throughout the meal. She would open her mouth and chew and swallow but it was as though she had forgotten how to serve herself. In December of 2015 we attended our last Bethel University "Festival of Christmas" together. The "Festival," an annual music concert, was always a favorite, preceded by a classic smorgasbord with Scandinavian treats. Retirees and active faculty and staff attend—many of them our friends, folks we'd sat with and talked with for two decades. That year, I asked one of the staff to seat us away from the group of retirees and current faculty and staff, so that I could feed her without embarrassing her or myself or distracting others. This was our last big ceremonial outing. I wore a suit and tie, and Candy had on nice slacks and sweater, and a fabric full-front bib that buttoned behind her neck to keep it on. A month earlier, we had Thanksgiving at our daughter's home, and photos show a tableful of happy, smiling family and Candy, eyes heavy-lidded, tired and confused.

We went out very seldom for meals in the last two years of her life. When we traveled, I would buy takeout, and feed her in our room, to avoid embarrassing her. Breakfasts were simple, often hot cereal, juice, and toast. I have tried to assess, over these months, whether I was embarrassed by her inability, perhaps embarrassed that others might think, "Who is that guy, and why is he treating her like that," or simply determined to help her get a meal concluded so we could move on with the day.

It's not unusual, I think, for caregivers to regard themselves as selfish or uncaring, even when they're not. After all, the caregiver is making the decisions in areas that used to be the other person's.

In her last fourteen months, all of this changed and became much more problematic. When she came home from transitional care, January 1, 2017, although she had been able to feed herself a little at the care center, within a month she was unable to do so. For all of 2017, I felt in a constant battle to get enough calories in her, and particularly protein so that her body could rebuild injured tissue. I failed, of course. I was battling her body's decline, and over the year she lost more than a hundred pounds.

Travel

We traveled pretty successfully for several years after 2008, the watershed year of her retirement. Alaska, Hawaii, travel to visit friends in Grand Marais and family in Spokane, we managed. We started the Na Pali Coast trail on Kauai; we hiked in Phoenix; we walked sections of the Superior Hiking Trail on the North Shore; we walked a misty, damp state park trail outside of Anchorage. Because she had worn an implanted defibrillator for more than 20 years, she always was "wanded" in a special security lane which let us through the airport with little difficulty. But by early 2014, our last flight to Spokane, the rules had changed, and she now needed to walk through a scanner, stop, lift her arms, and stay in place.

She couldn't do it, and she couldn't understand directions. I had to hold her hands while she went through an embarrassing patdown, trying to reassure her. That was our last flight.

In July 2014, the summer after I "fully" retired, I decided to act on a long-simmering problem. Where would we live our last years? Yes, we'd been settled in the Twin Cities for 20 years, the last ten in a home that was reasonably ready for aging people. Everything except the laundry was on the main floor, doors and halls were wide enough (we thought) for wheelchairs, and so on. But did I want to stay in St. Paul forever? No. I had always dreamed of having mountains on the horizon. So we made a "fish or cut bait" trip back to Spokane. Our visit also became part of a family reunion with Candy's brother, my brothers and my aunt and her family. We looked at places I'd love to live. And drove home. I realized near the end of the trip that I simply couldn't make this move: we had a support network, we had children and grandchildren in the Cities, and we would almost be starting fresh in Spokane. We'd been gone for more than 40 years.

But it was the travel itself that made it absolutely clear that I couldn't go. Candy had already been wearing Depends for months, by then. Somewhere in the middle of North Dakota, I realized that I needed to get her into dry ones, and it was miles from any rest stop. So there we are, off the freeway on an entrance ramp, she standing up between the car's open doors, pants down, while I struggle to get a wet brief off her, clean her, and get a clean side-tab brief on her, dress her, and get her back in the car. Clearly, I needed to plan better.

In December 2015, without hesitation our primary physician authorized a handicapped tag for the car. No long walks through the parking lot, her arm interlaced with mine to keep her balance.

Our worst travel experience, though, was our last road trip. We took a week away in early fall 2016, using our time-share points for a visit to Avon, Colorado. I'd learned that the first thing in travel planning was verifying the "family-friendly rest stops" along the way. I could walk Candy to the restroom (by this time, I needed to take her by the arm to keep her steady), get her into the restroom, change her, and get back to the car. We had some of the most beautiful country we'd ever been in all around us. A ride down Glenwood Canyon, following I-70 along the Colorado River through overhanging 1300- foot-high cliffs, may be the most awesome thirteen miles in the country.

On the way home, outside of Des Moines, she suddenly had an attack of diarrhea. I got to a rest stop within moments, grabbed my "go bag" from the back seat, walked her into the rest room, and in ten minutes got her clean and changed, brief, pants, and socks. The clothes went into a trash bag, sealed tight.

Illness

We had always supported each other when we were sick. I seldom was, for most of our lives, but Candy dealt with heart arrhythmia, with low thyroid, with migraines. We were lucky almost never to be ill at the same time. With the arrhythmia and thyroid, it was critical that she have low doses of several medications morning and evening. Too little, she had no energy; too much, she'd have erratic heartbeats. We managed.

But in her last several years, the number of illnesses seemed to increase. She was discouraged, sometimes deeply so. So was I. The worst moments were right after a bout of stomach flu in the winter of early 2016. She vomited in bed, and I got her to the bathroom, stripped her down, and watched in shock as she stood in front of the mirror, naked, and suffered an explosive diarrhea attack. She was completely confused and helpless, and seemed not to understand what was happening. I grabbed more towels, and got her clean again. I sat her in a chair wrapped in a blanket, stripped the bed, remade it, and laid her down, curled up. Then I got a tub of warm water, more towels, and rubber gloves, and cleaned the floor, the wall, the bathroom vanity, and then the bedroom carpet, the bedroom wall, and spot-cleaned the drapes. Then it was time for laundry.

In her last two years, she had several episodes like this, when she would wake up at night and vomit without warning. She was shocked and clearly frightened, even though she had no words to say so. I would get her changed, strip the bed, remake it, get her settled, and then start laundry, often at one or two in the morning. When this happened two nights running after we returned from Colorado (in mid-November 2016) I took her in to our clinic, where the doctor suggested she might have GERD, gastro-esophogeal reflux disease, and prescribed some antacids. The doctor suggested a change of diet. This helped for two days, and suddenly we had two nights of vomiting.

And of course Candy couldn't tell us what was wrong, or what was hurting. She had no words by this time, at all.

What I didn't comprehend was that this meant was that she was also vomiting up her medications. Those medications protected her from the heart arrhythmia she'd had since 1984. On the morning of November 22, six days after our initial visit to the clinic, as I was getting her ready to go to the clinic again, her defibrillator began to go off, shocking her some 20 times before doctors could get her stable. She collapsed in the hallway to the bedroom, and it took two EMT/paramedics to lift her, get her to an ambulance, and get her down to our local hospital. After time in the emergency room and admission to the hospital, she was stable. After a couple of days at home, suddenly, she was back in the emergency room, where doctors quickly found an inflamed gall bladder and pancreas.

It took more than a week to resolve this crisis, with me spending most of the days during that time with her, helping feed her, although nurses changed her. She was passive, medicated for pain, and quiet, almost withdrawn. We waited most of that time for the inflammation to go down before they could try a "less-invasive" procedure than gall bladder surgery. No one wanted her to suffer the pain and recovery of surgery, even if it was laparoscopic. She wouldn't know what was going on, so that everything would be alarming or painful. As she gained strength from good care, she seemed more able to track what was going on in the room. She was noticeably calmer when I was there with her, the nurses told me.

A hospitalization-level illness like this turns you inside out, and all your expectations are scattered. As we neared the end of the episode, with the endoscopy and procedure on the horizon, the "next thing" arose. She would not be able to go home easily, and the doctors recommended transitional care and rehabilitation. With the help of gracious social workers, we were able to find several good options, and the best one, quite miraculously, opened up. It was just a mile from where we lived on the north side of St. Paul, so that I could see her easily and spend time with her. After two or three days of increasing strength, some evaluation, a response to antibiotics, she was ready to be moved. At the last possible moment, a room opened, and a St. Paul fire department ambulance drove her through a below-zero snowstorm the ten or so miles to the care center.

Chapter 15

Uncoupling

If you're looking for a practical chapter in this book, this might be it. The "indignities" someone faces with dementia are identity-wounding, and they are emotionally perilous for caregivers. They force caregivers to develop some sort of emotional distance from the person they love in order to be effective at helping. Some of our modesty, our sense of appropriateness, our unity with this person must give way.

Through much of this process, though, we continue to treat those we care for as responsible, functioning men and women. But at some point, we likely are forced to stop, because they cease to be legally competent.

Three documents are critical for partners facing dementia. We had only one of them as Candy began to fail. We'd developed wills back in 1998, so had those in place. But we didn't have two documents we really needed: a health-care directive and a power of attorney document. Before Candy lost language altogether, she signed a health-care directive that enabled me to supervise her care and intervene if our health-care organization wanted procedures to which we hadn't agreed. Thankfully, that never came up.

I will say bluntly that our unpreparedness came from a failure of imagination. We simply didn't believe that Candy's condition could make it so that she was not competent to make decisions. And when I say "we," I mean it. Neither of us foresaw this, and I expect we deliberately did not want to face it.

The most important failure on our part was neglecting the power of attorney document. This document empowers someone to make a range of financial decisions on behalf of someone else. The scope may be narrow or broad. We didn't have one. Candy received a monthly Social Security check by direct deposit into our bank account, but we had a joint account, so my income went in there as well. Did we need to separate them? Yes.

I consulted with an attorney about how to proceed as she began to fail. She recommended—because Candy's ability to communicate was already seriously impaired—that I propose a "conservatorship" and a "guardianship" for Candy. This meant that I would be the "conservator" of her finances, authorized to make certain financial decisions, which the Ramsey County District Court would oversee. And I would also be her "guardian"— the phrase used is "guardianship of the person"—making sure of her health and daily well-being. In early 2016, after several months of filing and review, a court hearing accomplished this in about half an hour, with Candy sitting with the attorney in the courtroom. She could not respond to questions from the judge, and while she was curious about the hearing, appeared to have no understanding of what all this fuss was about.

"Conservatorship" meant a restructuring of our finances: from one family checking account to two, one a "Conservator" account for Candy; transferring money into that account from our family account; canceling one bank card (jointly held) and replacing it with two different cards, one for me and one for her; canceling joint credit cards and opening new accounts that were separate. The process also meant that I needed to account for all spending for Candy, and establish a baseline of funding for "maintenance" that included half of all our joint housing, food, and utility costs, and all costs related to her healthcare, clothing, and so forth. I continued to pay for most "joint" expenses, such as our homeowners association fees, insurance payments, transportation, from one account, and then reimburse "my" account from the conservatorship account of Candy's resources. At the end of the calendar year, I would have to present a computerized report enumerating all of this.

Anyone who's dealt with household accounts can imagine the paperwork that went into this transition. Any autopay or Electronic Fund Transfer information had to be changed for a number of vendors. This included new information sent to Social Security; to our healthcare provider for monthly premiums; to water, electrical, gas utilities; to our garbage collector. And on and on.

It also meant increased vigilance, even more than I'd practiced, to make sure that the proper accounts were charged or credited and documented over time.

Most of the assets in our lives were jointly held—a phrase attorneys use is "joint tenancy with right of survivorship," for some of the assets. As a practical matter, those would pass automatically to me at her death. Her will—I was the primary beneficiary, as she was mine—handled the few other assets held separately. Our home, one of our two cars, personal property such as furniture, and so forth, were jointly owned. Our retirement plans, insurance policies, and so forth also named each other as beneficiaries, so we didn't need to make changes in them.

In practical ways, I was "uncoupling," a process that certainly didn't make me feel good or supportive. I was for legal purposes separating our lives as a married couple from Candy's standing as an individual. She was now, in some respects, a "protected person" because of her disabling condition. I was now "Responsible Guy" pretty fully and with the authority of the

Ramsey County District Court behind me. And she was "not competent."

Emotionally, it made me aware of how fragile support could be for someone with dementia. We had our savings, investments, and a home, and no debt. But Candy's real income was about $14,000 a year from Social Security without investments or our retirement plans. "Fixed" expenses, including utilities and taxes, amounted to most of that. Since we were together, we could manage and have some reserve.

"Guardianship" meant that I was responsible for her "person," her health, safety, and daily well-being. Much of what I've shared in this book highlights how I cared for her. But some surprises showed up. For instance, the shift to "Depends" undergarments because of her incontinence amounted to about a thousand dollars in 2016.

I had no idea until late December 2016 about the resources a "hospice" situation opened up. A nurse specializing in hospice and a social worker with our health plan met with me as Candy recovered in the hospital from her endoscopy. Between Medicare and our health plan, Candy's medical expenses, including equipment such as a hospital bed and the supplies such as briefs, wipes, lotions, and even her prescriptions, would be covered. I discovered that weekly nursing visits and twice-weekly personal care visits were included in hospice care. All we had to do was keep on paying our premiums for health insurance and Medicare. We had decided a long time ago that we would prefer to be at home—both of us—rather than hospitalized or "nursing homed," and I took up the responsibility for full-time care.

I was now nurse, dietitian, cook, personal care attendant, and estate and property manager. Somehow "husband" and "lover" took lower priority. Uncoupling.

Chapter 16

Real Time: Facebook—Hospice at Home

After hospitalization in late 2016, Candy came home for a "hospice in home." We put up a hospital bed in our second bedroom and arranged the furniture to accommodate a "lift" for her. For the first time in 46 years, we were sleeping apart.

Thursday, January 5, 2017: First Days Home

Candy is doing well at home. Her appetite continues good, and is, I think, improving. She enjoyed a fair-sized piece of lasagna last night, and because I decided "eat salad first," she had a small salad for the first time in weeks, and seemed to enjoy all of it.

We had our first home health aide visit (part of hospice) yesterday, and Erica gave Candy a sponge bath, gave me good advice, and will be with us again on Friday. We finally got a stand-lift--it takes you from sitting on the edge of a bed or from a wheelchair, lifts you gently to a standing position, and then sits you down gently again. Its advantage over a sling lift (what's called a "full lift") is that it encourages patients to maintain leg strength (weight-bearing), and in the process gently stretches tendons and muscles that never get used if someone is sitting all the time. I got Candy's transport chair adjusted yesterday--somehow all my Allen wrenches have become invisible, but a neighbor handed me a box with thirty different sizes, so we're good.

We were not without adventures. While trying to do a transfer yesterday morning "by hand," with a transfer belt, we both fell, ending up on the carpet. It was more of a "down easy," but it made me glad I had the full lift to get her up into her chair. When I talked to the aide later, she reminded me that accidents happen; I responded that stupid doesn't need to happen, and that I was being stupid by not focusing on one simple thing at a time. We're both okay, and she wasn't traumatized--the virtue of fading memory, I guess. I was embarrassed, and I will try to remember, even though, as we know, guilt is only a good *short-term* motivator.

Saturday, January 17, 2017: Making Adjustments

It's just below zero right now, with a high of 9 today! We've had several good days, although I keep having to be mindful of what we'll have for a meal so I make sure Candy can and will eat healthy. Her appetite continues good, and she is swallowing well. Yesterday's visit with a home health aide from hospice introduced us to Heather, who bathed Candy and washed her hair. I could tell she appreciated the skin-to-skin friendliness. When I looked in on her at 4 a.m. this morning, she opened her eyes, smiled, and sang wordlessly to me. I stroked her face, kissed her, and talked her back to sleep. I'm still working to get the house arranged so it "works" and doesn't feel cluttered. Adding several large pieces of equipment to a small room means that the "normal" furniture has to go or be repurposed or at least stored.

Monday, January 23, 2017: Anniversaries

Over the Facebook years, I've posted a number of times about life events. Last year's post, on this date, was about our

45th anniversary, and in it, I thanked the communities of faith of which we'd been a part for helping us learn how to be really, deeply married. I'm renewing that today.

We are at the beginning of a new week, and I'm trying to remind myself, with my second cup of coffee, that God's mercies are new every morning. Candy is in her hospital bed in our "second bedroom." She's been awake at least once this morning, just before my alarm went off at 4, and I heard her singing in that low-voiced cry from her room. Wordless, it is at a constant pitch that seems to say, "Is anyone there? Can you come to me? I don't understand. I am frightened."

I went in and talked with her, checked her brief, adjusted the support for her feet, and turned out the light so she could sleep again, and she has. I'll check on her in a little bit, but because today's our anniversary, I won't be in a hurry to get her up. I'm not sure what our celebration will be tonight, but if I can, it will include a Culver's ice cream sundae. A word of thanks: to our Rice Creek Church friends, for the bag full of containers of spaghetti and meatballs, and garlic bread, and salad makings that Randy and Pam delivered yesterday. Supper was instantaneous last night, because of you. One less thing to deal with.

February 17, 2017: Routines and Love

Two weeks ago we celebrated (well, *I* did) 46 years of "married."

Candy and I first dated in October, 1967, four months out of high school, and within weeks I thought, "Wow....I want to know her. She's fascinating, she's different, she's shy, she's smart....and she laughs at my jokes and finds *me* fascinating. So"....I'll skip the sappy parts. They were conventional, they were romantic, and so forth. Fast forward. We were two ordinary kids, very capable, learning how to live together and work together. Normal amounts of shy, normal amounts of modest, etc.

We're 67 now. When I waken her about 7, there's a routine that—if followed to the letter—enables me to get her dressed and out into the kitchen in about 30-35 minutes. A drop of Systane in each eye, which she hates, because she hates anyone putting anything in her eyes. Raise the bed to nearly full height. Pull the covers back, and change the brief—clean brief at hand, wipes, barrier cream, gloves on. Untab the briefs, pull her gently toward you, step around the bed, reach over her and use the draw sheet to turn her gently on her side, shift her legs so that the "top" leg is in front of the "bottom leg," so she's not balanced on her hip, step back to the other side, remove the old brief, use wipes to clean her, apply barrier cream, lay out the new brief, tucking the tabs under her, gently roll her onto her back, step around the bed, pull the brief up, more wipes and barrier cream, lift her knees gently to get the brief situated right, tab up. Put clean sweatpants on her, which you won't be able to secure until she's in the stand lift. Get the stand lift and transport chair situated, get the lift sling around her, help her sit up, and raise her in the lift. From there, once she's settled in her transport chair, you have other tasks: nightgown off over the head; anti-perspirant applied to her underarms (if you don't, you'll have skin issues inside a week); shirt/sweater; brush her hair; clean her glasses and put them on. Add socks.

In the kitchen and at the table: it's my job to make sure she eats and gains strength. That means I plan every mouthful. I make sure she has enough to drink; if she sneezes with food in her mouth—common with dementia—I make sure to catch the food in a terry towel.

When she's back in bed, pull the legs up on her sweatpants, take off her socks, roll her gently to one side, and check on the quarter-size pressure wounds on her calves and the dime-sized ones on her heels. Take a gauze square, apply some wound cleaner, and *very gently* apply it to the area where two or three levels of skin and tissue have died, leaving an open wound a sixteenth-inch deep. Gently apply a dab of Medi-Honey to the area, add a gauze square, and wrap the heel or the calf with a gauze wrap. Tape gently with micropore tape. Pull her pants legs down. Replace socks, gently. These wounds will take six months to heal.

Here's my point. Unless you are prepared to exclude that "in sickness and in health" and "until death do us part" stuff, marriage will lead you to some serious challenges that will get you well beyond modest, and competent, and shy. Yes, we've had years of overwhelming delight, and celebration, and laughter, and friendship, and deep affection. We've had naked and we've had dress-up. We've had romance that smoldered, and romance that exploded. I'm not complaining about the way the role's evolved.

People tell me I'm doing pretty well. I don't know how capable I am at doing it, or how long (for a long time, I hope) I can continue to do it. I don't know that I ever thought about preparing for these kinds of things. Use the inevitability of them in your life to gauge whether there's a person you'd be willing to love and serve *to that degree*. Because if you live long enough, and if you are extraordinarily lucky, that's what marriage grows into.

Chapter 17

Real Time: Facebook—Love in Stories

Monday, March 27, 2017

Yvette is giving Candy a wash-up down the hall in her bedroom, and I'm working at the kitchen table in case I need to assist. Yvette is about 5'5", maybe, and might be 100 pounds. She's very professional, but this is her first time helping Candy, and so I want to be here if she needs me. It makes for a good opportunity to pull out the laptop.

I was musing Saturday evening about a little sit-down I had with son Peter earlier in the day. He'd come by to drop something off, and asked an interesting question that he prefaced with a story. When he and Em were growing up, one of them asked how Candy and I had met and gotten married. This was not a story I think I ever heard Candy tell them, so I was amused and interested to hear it remembered from someone at 10 years old or so.

What Candy told them was that we had started to go out together in college, and I kept asking her out—coffee, walks on campus, talking. At some point she realized I really cared about her and that this could grow into something serious—which I think sort of amazed and unnerved her. Did she really want to go out with and establish a serious relationship with this rather mild and apparently super-conventional guy? Was she willing to settle for "mild" and "dependable," and "bright" and "weird"? Then she told them that she had heard a song one night that sort of cemented that thought in place. We actually heard the band perform this song—I think we were over in Moscow at the U of Idaho with Curt Kirkemo and Don Beattie and Steve Herzog and Scott Wallin—the whole Whidbey Island group that seemed so much more sophisticated than we were. I can date it, although somewhat tentatively, as late October, 1967. It would have been, I imagine, about our third or fourth date. The song was The Association's "Cherish," which has lines like "Cherish is the word I use to describe / All the feeling that I have hiding here for you inside."

All that's okay. I'm a lot less comfortable now with those lines like "You don't know how many times I've wished that I could / Mold you into someone who could / Cherish me as much as I cherish you." That notion of "mold you into someone" seems fundamentally to disrespect the other person. Hey, we were 18, besotted, and that's the way it was. And she realized that I was interested in her for her, and not for me.

But what Pete focused on when we talked on Saturday was how that myth of the good guy persistently hanging in there until the girl comes around and recognizes "He's the One" had affected him. And maybe that myth of the persistent nice guy whose behavior calls out the virtues in the shy or wild or rebellious girl or woman, too. So the story Candy seems to have told them is, in some ways, a traditional romantic narrative—boy meets girl, boy falls for girl, boy pursues girl, girl eventually realizes "*He's the One*," reciprocates affection, and so on. How many 70's and 80's and 90's movies adopted this plot? Except, as Pete pointed out, it's a plot for the movies because it happens so seldom that we'll pay good money to see this sort of everybody's dream played out with attractive actors. It taps into all of our *"I Want This to Be True"* emotions. So, he asked me, was it true?

And I told him it was probably true from his mother's perspective, but not from mine. My perspective on our courtship was that it was a lot more tenuous and filled with anxiety than that. She told me years later that her parents had really wanted a six-two blond Scandinavian Lutheran for her, not a five-ten dark-haired Scots-Irishman of uncertain Protestantism. I had some barriers to overcome. I thought she was wonderful—pretty, shy, bright, insightful, funny—different from me in all the right ways, and like me in all the right ones, too. And I had no idea what I'd do if she decided on someone else. I thought she was "the right one," and I got lucky. But I never had that CSN "helplessly hoping" *"She's the one"* thing going. In my generation of siblings, for the five boys who made it to adulthood, there are 11 marriages or long-term relationships—and since brother Tom and I are still on our first wives, that should suggest something.

Life is complicated, and marriage is not easy. It has nothing to do with how well educated you are, or how bright—in three generations, the Sherry men and women have a couple of doctorates, several master's degrees, and all graduated from good colleges. Sometimes, as Art Garfunkel sings, you're *"looking for the right one"* for a long time. My father divorced his first wife—back in Massachusetts—and married my mother. His father divorced his first wife—my grandmother. Dysfunctional relationships are not a foreign concept in the family. That myth of the persistent partner whose faithfulness evokes hidden virtues in the other person, leading to a radical repentance? Probably played a part in sustaining some of those mismatches. Not true or honest then, and dubious today.

So I wasn't "hopelessly in love" during our courtship. But then we got married, and I was.

Chapter 18

Spirituality

I have been writing about our lives as a couple with sort of side-long references to our faith and beliefs. But I'm aware readers come from different traditions and maybe no faith tradition at all. Here I want to be more direct without excluding anyone.

So let me be explicit. I'm a Christian, steadily if thinly and ignorantly Protestant throughout my formative years, and more deeply and consciously so since college. And while the particulars of our spiritual experience were really important to us, what may be useful to the general reader is to consider that most human beings seem to share both moral values and a sense of the transcendent. You might call them "horizontal" and "vertical" concerns. We are certainly aware of the need for honorable, caring relationships with one another. We are simultaneously aware of and perhaps long for more participation in a life beyond our own, lives with meaning beyond the sixty or seventy years most of us have. For instance, almost all of us seek to leave a legacy or an impact on the world—even though we ourselves will not be a part of that world. We may be meat, but we appreciate the stars.

Membership, participation in a group of like-minded people, enables this. Our own lives and beliefs are strengthened, for good or for ill. Candy and I found groups of like-minded men and women to join that renewed us, cared for us, opened opportunities for service and things to believe.

Candy's increasing memory loss, language loss in particular, affected her sense of herself and her relationship with God in dramatic ways.

As I wrote earlier, Candy was raised in a Lutheran home, went through confirmation as a teenager, and was active in her church's youth groups and activities. In this, she is like many young men and women, influenced by older adherents to a faith tradition, and finding in their example a pattern or model to follow. During our college years, she built a relationship with an older couple who became very important to her, modeling a mature Christian marriage, facing difficulties (like children with disabling conditions) with grace, humor, and love. They were people full of humor, wit, advice, and encouragement; after sixty years of marriage, they have recently been parted, but the husband remains, as steady and good a man as you will find anywhere.

During our sophomore year, they encouraged Candy to attend a weekly prayer gathering in someone's home in our college town. It was at the beginning of a surge of charismatic religious experiences in the Pacific Northwest that cut across Protestant and Catholic traditions. The result was that her faith, her experience of trust in God, became deeper, more personal, and surprisingly more private. She had had spiritual experiences that led to a deeper devotional life: more Bible study, more prayer, greater openness to what she perceived as God's leading.

Candy entered into these experiences, not without some hesitation, and gradually. For much of the second half of our sophomore year, I think, she attended weekly.

I would say I was still on the outside of the Christian experience in those days. I had been a consistent church attender, but incidents in my childhood led me at the very least to distrust what the church proclaimed about God's goodness and love. I listened to her share about her experiences in this renewal movement with considerable skepticism. I thought they were mostly emotional, likely the product of manipulation by others, and something I wanted to stay clear of. She invited me to attend several times, and I can't remember that I ever did. And if I did, I'm pretty sure I've buried the event as deeply as I could.

You could say we were divided in this: I thought myself the more "intellectual" Christian, focusing on the pastoral message at church. She valued more than I did the messages communicated in the liturgy, the hymns and worship songs. This showed up in our private lives, too. Even after I committed myself to follow Christ, midway through our senior year in college and shortly before we married, I remained seriously and privately skeptical of some of her spiritual experiences. I'm sure that affected how much she shared with me.

But consider the results of her beliefs and trust in God.

At her memorial service, almost a half century after those experiences, Emily and Peter shared, Em about Candy's encouragement and support for a 1996 Belize summer mission trip. She told Em that she was praying for her the words God speaks to Joshua: "Have I not commanded you? Be strong and courageous. Do not be afraid; do not be discouraged, for the Lord your God will be with you wherever you go."

Pete commented about Candy's love for words and The Word, the Bible: "Many teachers and professors have made me memorize facts, figures, history, and even Scripture throughout my life, but mom taught me to memorize Scripture because it was life – and she lived this passage, and so many others like it – in a way that was impossible to ignore, and impossible to not respect, regardless of one's faith persuasion.

"And as I think back on her life, and on the many things she taught me from an early age, particularly about words, and the Word, my Christian faith tradition also reminds me that death, even death through slow decline, does not have the final word. Thanks be to God."

My children had the experience of growing up with a mother who taught them about the presence of transcendence in their lives, and the reality that a transcendent God could be "with us" in our daily lives. She never wavered in believing this, confident that in our daily lives we were "inhabited" by the Holy Spirit the New Testament promises.

And I will add, to be honest, she kept me accountable by asking, as a matter of routine, what God was doing in my thinking and my life.

And at the same time, she was struggling for decades, over and over again in her daily experience, to be obedient to the things she believed the Bible taught. She struggled to maintain daily habits of personal devotion, like Bible reading and prayer. She struggled not to be afraid or to find ways through the financial challenges of our married life. She fretted about being critical of others, and "cattiness" in her comments about others. She struggled with very tangible issues, like her weight, her appearance.

Near the time she was diagnosed with aphasia, she had gained a significant amount of weight, and felt herself out of control in her eating. Over four or five years after the diagnosis, she worked hard at losing that weight, going from size 20 slacks to size 10, and losing perhaps sixty pounds. On her 5'9" frame, it was dramatic. And then, after 2010, as she lost words more and more, she gained much of it again, despite lots of morning walks, water aerobics when she could, and time at the gym with me. She found herself facing, in this specific way, what the neurologists call "disinhibition."

"Disinhibition" is slippage of what might be called the "No, I shouldn't do that" element of our thinking. It's the inability to stop what those around us might call "socially inappropriate" behavior. For some, both men and women, it leads to heightened, almost compulsive sexual behavior. In others, to eating or compulsive exercise.

Against these impulses, Candy prayed, writing her devotional diary as a series of prayers focused around her daily Bible reading. She knew she was losing words, sometimes talking about her "word problems," or her "thinking problems." Again and again, she clung to a few promises she felt God had given her from her reading. Two stood out to her over several years, the first from the apostle John's good news. At a crisis point early in Jesus' ministry, many desert him, unable to confront their culturally-conditioned expectations. Jesus asks the disciples if they're leaving too, and Peter responds, "Lord, to whom shall we go? You have the words of eternal life." The second was from the Book of Proverbs: "Trust in the Lord with all your heart, and do not rely on your own insight. In all your ways acknowledge Him, and He will make your paths straight."

Those entries show her struggling, calling out to God, longing for reassurance, and at the same time clinging to promises years-long in the midst of what she perceived as silence.

Especially in the months before she lost all language, she talked with me about how she wanted to trust God all the way to the end, and believed he would "make her path straight." And often as she lay on her hospital bed in hospice, I would lean over her and repeat that verse to her, arms around her, whispering quietly, our heads together.

For many years, we attended a small church a few miles away from us, bypassing much larger churches where we would have been part of a crowd. We sat in the back, in part because I wanted to be able to get her to the bathroom, and in part because for the last year or so we were there she might well fall asleep on my shoulder. People understood. When she could, she would stand and wordlessly sing the tune of hymns or worship songs, smiling at me and clearly enjoying melody, rhythm, the energy of forty or sixty people united. She might find herself falling asleep with the pastor's message, but the music awakened her at some level deeper than words.

And she deeply enjoyed the greetings, the smiles, the hugs from our church friends. Many understood that the warmth of a community can be at the heart of our sense of "church," of what it means to express love as part of our faith. Her very last outing, a Christmas Eve service a month before she passed away, was the first time in our church in a year. And people clustered around for a hug, a kiss, talking gently with her.

We have to face the fact that an illness like this--whether it's Alzheimer's that leaves many faculties intact, or a dementia that slowly robs one of motion, of reason, of memory, of communication—also transforms our sense of the spiritual and of ourselves as spiritual beings. For Candy, I think it increased her sense of intellectual uncertainty, of confusion about the world. It led her to distrust herself and even to distrust her memories of what she knew and had believed for years, things that expressed meaning and purpose. What lasted the longest was the sense of being held, of being enfolded in love. I hope I do not deceive myself when I remember that when she was discouraged we sat together on the couch and I reminded her of all she had accomplished in the lives of her children, grandchildren, friends and students. And of how much I loved her.

Chapter 19

Terror

There are moments in caregiving when you go from the ordinary—it's never boring, and often exhausting, but it's "normal"—to terror in a split second. The first pressure wound, what we used to call a "bed sore." You realize that that dark spot isn't just a bruise—well, it is, but it's black in the center, surrounded by purple—and you understand over a day or two that that tissue is dead, and the skin will open, and a level of tissue will be lost. And it will, you learn, take months to heal. The first one occurred in April 2017, during my first "respite," while Candy was at a local care center for five days. We had been in "hospice at home" for three months, and the hospice program (collaborative between our health provider and Medicare) provided for this. I'd used the first two days of "respite" to get three stents installed in heart arteries, and then three days to drive to Grand Marais and begin the first draft of this book. When I got Candy home and in bed, almost the first thing I saw were black dime-sized spots on her heels. The care center hadn't followed the nurse's directions on supporting her legs and feet. I called the nurse, who called the care center. *Oops,* they said. *We're sorry. It wasn't on the notes the nurse gave us.*

They wouldn't heal until almost September. They won't kill you, but they're sites for opportunistic infections, and they consume your system trying to heal them. When the body is slowing down, when it can't get the protein or nourishment it needs, healing takes months.

As a caregiver you find yourself constantly on the alert for such things, until you have a routine of "normal" to check circulation on your partner, positioning pillows and blankets to prop her up, relieve pressure on feet, calves, hips, buttocks. You try to protect her.

I knew things were getting worse as we came to later November 2017. Our nurse and care attendant were relieved when I got away for a Thanksgiving respite, and Candy was in the care center only a mile away, where she'd been twice before. She had lost more than eighty pounds over the year, despite three meals daily and morning and afternoon "Boost" drinks with extra protein. As always, this care center's performance was outstanding.

But back home in December, three days before Christmas, as I was transferring her from her chair back to bed, as I took her left arm a quarter-sized patch of skin tore along one edge, leaving a gap a quarter-inch wide. She winced, and then looked at it, and at me. I was stunned. What was this?! I had taken her arm to guide her from sitting to lying down, and I TORE HER SKIN.

I called the nurse as soon as I'd wrapped it lightly in gauze.

Yes, she said. *Remember how I told you her skin was breaking down? This is it.*

Wait, I thought. *I thought we were using lotion to help that.* I asked her.

No, she said. *Rich, Candy is terminal. This is what happens. Try to move it back in place, gently, then wrap it lightly.*

And I remember she'd used "terminal" in our last hospice review, done every quarter at first, then every sixty days.

Over the next three weeks, until mid-January, the skin on her arm became more fragile, tearing or shredding almost with any contact or pressure. By her last week, it would have taken a dollar bill to cover the tears on her left forearm. I tried to work around it, arm under her, using the draw sheet to turn her, caring for new pressure wounds near the base of her spine and where her hip bones—now without fat and with muscles atrophied—were acutely sensitive to pressure. I became familiar with "Stage 2" and "Stage 3" wounds where skin layers are gone and raw tissue is visible. You try to find a position every half hour or hour that relieves the pressure and encourages circulation. All day and into the night.

And try to believe that small amounts of oxycodone, tiny sips of water, droppersful, will ease this. If she takes more, you know she'll choke. You try to believe that what you are doing makes a difference.

And in the end, a week later on that bright Saturday morning, while Kathryn read a psalm to her, she slipped away.

Chapter 20

Real Time: Facebook—Afterwards

March 2018: A House Barely Inhabited

At Candy's memorial service on Friday, February 2, our pastor, Toni Schwabe, read something I'd written. I didn't trust myself to be able to get through it. Here are two paragraphs as a way to start thinking about what's going on now.

Most of you here have very different perceptions of Candy than her family have. In the last eleven years, since she was diagnosed, she has lost the ability to communicate with words, and we have watched memory and abilities stripped away. She handed over her work as a reference librarian, her driver's license, and her mastery of the kitchen.

But we knew her before that as a woman full of energy and full of adventure. She made places "home," wherever we were, whether it was a graduate school cinder-block-wall apartment, a small Kentucky town, or an eight-week "vacation" in Minneapolis, rural Connecticut, or Los Angeles. She planned adventures to California, and Texas, trips to family in Virginia and Spokane, and the "big adventures" of two weeks in England and Scotland, a cruise to Alaska, and a week in Hawaii. For us, home is where she was, because home is not a place, but people.

"For us, home is where she was, because home is not a place, but people."

I think I believe that now, but all of you surely recognize that there is a downside to operating that way. When the people are gone, nowhere you are feels quite like home. My half-sisters Lorraine Young and Sally Glinski know what I'm talking about—both have lost husbands, one many years ago, one recently. The house may stay the same, or change, but something essential, a joist running down the middle of the house, what some carpenters call a "bearer," is gone. It's one of the heaviest beams in the house, often three 2x12s nailed together with a further foot-wide piece of plywood between them. In some houses, it's one long steel beam, resting on steel jack posts from end to end of the house. Everything goes on top of it. In metaphor, it structured and supported your day, your schedule, your meals, your cleaning, your rest, your conversation, your belonging. I am still working all of that out, because the bearer is gone.

This last week I have been packing clothes to go to Goodwill or to a new for-profit, SimpleRecycling, which picks up with our alternate-week recycling. Forty pairs of shoes, all perfectly usable, business, hiking, walking, dress, winter. The tallest heels are two inches, because we were nearly the same height, and she never wanted to be taller than I was. Ten coats, eight for winter in various sizes, and I remember her holding my hand in all of them. Forty shirts or blouses, two dozen sweaters, dresses for all seasons (and lengths), six jacket and skirt suit combinations. Sweat pants and Danskin lounge pants for around the house, when the nurses told me, "Look, this works, and it's easy, and they look nice," and they were right. Two closets are empty, and a third and fourth nearly so, and they were the overflow—coats in one, summer things in the other. I remember her wearing that Washington State University sweatshirt in 1970, engagement ring on her hand, laughter bursting out in autumn and a wedding four months away.

Opening every closet, putting things on the bed, sorting, stuffing or folding them into an oversize garbage bag. It feels like things are humming along smoothly, and then—it *is* March in Minnesota—it's like driving into a pothole that'll tear your wheel off. You know it's there, you know it's coming if you take that road, and then you're in it, and your stomach drops out. The lurch of emotion sinks into you, and you ask, "What did I break this time?"

Some things Em can wear—a Land's End long down coat, worn a dozen times, perfect for this winter. Some are for others—heavy flannel shirts sent to sister-in-law Karla and niece Katie. Candy's Bethel-logo Land's End down vest is helping Katie through a Spokane winter. Some things I will not part with, like the mittens my mother made for us, one "His," one "Hers," and one "Ours" made for holding hands, an oversize with two wristlets for walking together on winter nights at college. Odditymall calls theirs "Smitten Mittens": Mom knitted them for us as winter came on in the cold of 1968, and we laughed, and we wore them, Christmas-red with green lettering knitted in. "Ours."

It is odd to pack away in oversize garbage bags the clothes I remember her wearing, though the memories are now years old. They are in all sizes, from the "10" she wore seven years ago to the "20" before the final descent sixteen months ago. I pack them—fifteen bags, so far, two just of coats—in the Subaru, and off to Goodwill, two miles away. Every one of them says, "She's gone, and she's not coming back." More ruthlessly, a voice says, "She died, you know, and you buried her. Don't look for her before the Resurrection." And a small person inside is still dis-believing all of this. That person is clinging to routine, and sched-ule, and a place barely inhabited any more.

Chapter 21

First Steps Out

In late April 2018, I began dating. How do you do this, after half a century? I was inept in high school, had few dates before I met Candy, and now was wondering what was next in my life.

How very 21st century. I went online, signed up for a dating site, "OurTime.com," and had coffee with two women, a couple of weeks apart. We introduced ourselves. The second date was the last one, because I met Margie.

Some of my friends were scandalized, I think. (One of my brothers has told me that my brothers and sisters-in-law all celebrated.) Months later, when Margie and I met another couple who'd known Candy and me well, one asked (as I remember it), "How can you date someone else so soon? How can you write about loving Candy and date someone else at the same time?"

These were questions I was asking myself. Margie had lost her husband to cancer more than a decade earlier, and for her and her children, Tom was still both a real remembered person and an icon of "husband-and-father." And Margie answered my friends, "You never stop loving the one you lost."

And I told them that I had been grieving Candy's loss every day for ten years. And loving her at the same time.

A phenomenon I've learned about more recently, "ambiguous loss," is what I was experiencing. Pauline Boss writes about it in *Loving Someone Who Has Dementia.* For ten years, I was watching the person I loved most in the world, the closest friend, the most intimate, fade away. The whole of our relationship was dissolving, beach sand slipping away underfoot, every wave. She's still there, and yet she's not. You love her, and every intimate moment has less and less real relationship in it. You remember, and she does not. In the end, you find yourself remembering for her. And you keep faith, because, after all, you love her and you signed on to "until death parts us."

And it did. I don't think I felt "released" until that dream I wrote about later, in July of 2018. Until then, as much as I enjoyed getting to know Margie, I was still watching myself, standing on the sidelines, and wondering if what I was doing was insensitive, was a betrayal, was simply cold-blooded. More of that in a few pages, reader.

Chapter 22

Real Time: Facebook—Anniversaries

June 4, 2018: A Birthday Absence

Today, June 4th, Candy would have been 69 years old. And this is the first birthday in half a century we haven't been together. My emotions surprise me a little. Around our home, and even when I'm out, shared memories surround me. When I pull a CD out to play in the car, these were all songs we listened to together. Some of them—Susan Ashton, and some others—I never would have heard except that she played them. Her bike still hangs in the garage, lofted up, although mine is on the floor, readied for whatever. The dishes she inherited from her mother and grandmother are in the corner cabinet I finished in our first years in Kentucky. The counted cross-stitch that my mother began and Candy finished, listing all the grandchildren and great-grandchildren, hangs over my bed, as it has for the fourteen years we've lived here. Her presence is in some measure still here.

I have always been attracted to Tennyson's "Ulysses," which has Tennyson's Victorian take on the Greek hero. Ulysses' comment that "I am a part of all that I have met" is one I can affirm.

But Ulysses isn't saying that everything he met affected him—no, what he's saying is that other peoples' lives were different because *they met him*. Candy had that ability. My life with Candy enriched and changed me, as it did so many of our friends. Our children reflect her thoughtful and compassionate parenting, shown in many of the pictures I have of her. When you watch her with Pete and Em, she is leaning in, alongside, encouraging, smiling. In other pictures, people cluster around her, little children bring delight to her eyes, and she to them.

The last birthdays we had together were challenging. She was limited in what she could do, in how she could communicate, even in understanding what all the fuss was about. Last year, especially, as she was at home in hospice, was especially hard. The kids visited and Pete brought a plant to brighten her room. A day or so after her birthday, I wrote about how thin she was, and how discouraged I was about being unable to feed her enough to keep her weight up. I wrote:

> I was distressed at bedtime last night, reflecting on how little Candy had eaten at supper. And then I thought back to breakfast, with a full bowl of homemade oatmeal, and lunch, with a good cup of tomato soup, and some crackers, and some applesauce. Supper wasn't the only meal of the day. One of the gifts we have is to take a longer view, and remember.

Caregiving engages us in an effort not to deny the world and live in a fantasy. Things may get better, but "better" is likely to be temporary. Instead, we are challenged to understand a longer view.

Memories of those we love—those present with us today, and those who have gone on before us—link us across space and time. When we recall them, we honor the way they've changed our lives, their impact, often for eternity. And we recall their courage, their kindness, and their longings. It's not wrong to quote Ulysses' memorable lines: We may be "Made weak by time and fate, but strong in will/ To strive, to seek, to find, and not to yield." The memories of those we love can help us "not to yield."

When I think of her, I almost never think of this last year. Instead, I remember her courage, her love for God and for all of us, the way she poured herself out for others in seeking God, her laughter, her smile, her laughing, deep-blue eyes.

Chapter 23

Real Time: Facebook—Dream

July 27, 2018

I don't remember my dreams. Or perhaps I remember very few, and those tend toward the striking. Last night, though.

Today is six months since Candy slipped away. And honestly, I haven't been focusing on that anniversary, and it wasn't until mid-morning today that I even recalled the date.

In my dream, Candy and I are at home, and I need to take her into the hospital. It isn't frantic, but purposeful, serious, important, and I think I must be working to try to overcome some obstacles, but I can't recall any of them. I can't remember the journey there. She is in a wheelchair or transport chair, and I can recall getting into the hospital through sliding doors, and up the elevator to a doctor's office. I don't know of any doctor's office anywhere like this, walls of off-white, lights indirect. And Candy herself similarly wears an off white or a cream-colored outfit, pants and tunic, one I've never seen. She is silent, as she has been the last three or four years, and she can't leave her chair, as she could not for all of this last year.

What I remember most about my image of her in this dream is that she is young, and she is smiling. She is as beautiful and quietly full of life as she ever was. It is not the lips-parted smile just before a laugh, just that shy, impish, quiet smile I loved for decades. It tells you that you share something, and also that she finds the moment, for some reason, full of humor. This last year, as she steadily lost weight, her face also became almost expressionless. I do not look at photos I took of her this last year, for all of them give me the sense that either the Candy I loved so long is already gone, or that she is imprisoned there. But the dream is not like that.

In the waiting room, a doctor enters—again, strangely, in an off-white lab coat. I have no sense of his face, but after a few minutes' conversation with me, of which I cannot recall one word, he steps over to Candy's chair. She turns to look at me, with no sense of apprehension or alarm, and he takes both her hands. And suddenly, he is folding her clothes, and she is not there at all.

And I wake up.

I really resist people interpreting my dreams for me, and I am reluctant to force meaning into things like this. I will be content to let whatever meaning there is in this unfold in the days ahead. But I find the shape of this interesting, and its timing. At the end of the day after this dream, the only sense I have is of "Good-bye."

Chapter 24

Real Time: Facebook—Gentle Treatment

July 2018

It's been a great month. And I've learned some things about where I am in recovering from Candy's illness and death. At least two observations.

First, I hadn't realized consciously how much I have been The Responsible Guy, and how easily that becomes The Guy Who Steps In. The difference is that the first guy is dependable, and the second one can be annoying and intrusive. For seven or eight years I've been the partner who plans, who takes things into account, who gets us through airports, who remembers to pack the hair dryer, the medications, the hats, the gloves, and at the end, the guy responsible for buying bras and panties and making sure they fit, and making sure we have Enough of whatever is essential. I've also been the guy tending wounds, and cleaning up after bathroom accidents, and all that. Sort of a comprehensive "Guy in Charge of Everything," right down to making sure the soup isn't too hot and your partner's nails are clipped so she won't scratch herself.

But when you're surrounded by absurdly competent and energetic people, perhaps The Responsible Guy needs to change his repertoire. And my family is full of competent and energetic people. The Guy Who Steps In can sit down and enjoy things. No one's writing, as far as I can see, about how caregivers recover from this "You know, you're a pain in the neck" problem. Maybe I'm the only one who needs to be told, "Chill."

Second, unnoticed, is how much of my day and life had been active on behalf of Candy—in fact, how much of my life had been sort of "active waiting," corresponding to "active listening." But what it's meant is that it's been difficult to imagine moving forward, because for the last five years or so, especially, I could only count on the time between 4 and 6 in the morning to do any sustained work. That's meant short essays and Facebook reflections, the kind of thinking that I could manage in short chunks. Now, vistas of time open up, and I find myself sort of struggling to find direction and energy. Responsible Guy tends to be short-term and immediate-focused, because he has to be.

In some ways, recovering from this means re-establishing autonomy and redefining interdependence, not unlike those adolescent tasks we all face. Somehow, you start Separate Life when you're in college, still connected to the family tree, but branching, leafing in new directions. The roots and the attachment are there, but the direction changes. Same deal, except I'm 69, not 18.

I'm reminded of Tolkien's "Leaf by Niggle," as Niggle comes into Niggle's Parish and begins to walk toward the mountains. New adventures, all connected.

But Niggle, an undisciplined painter with great imagination, had needed both time in the workhouse (discipline) and the hospital (healing) first, as well as "gentle treatment." There's a lovely scene near the middle of "Leaf by Niggle," as Niggle hears the

First and Second Voices discussing his care. He is recovering from exhaustion.

'What do you propose?'

'I think it is a case for a little gentle treatment now,' said the Second Voice.

Niggle thought that he had never heard anything so generous as that Voice. It made Gentle Treatment sound like a load of rich gifts, and a summons to a King's feast. Then suddenly Niggle felt ashamed. To hear that he was considered a case for Gentle Treatment overwhelmed him, and made him blush in the dark. It was like being publicly praised, when you and all the audience knew that the praise was not deserved.[2]

The past month has been "gentle treatment," and good counsel, which have helped me see some of these things more clearly. As I began, it's been a great month. Margie is a great part of "gentle treatment," and I'm laugh-out-loud grateful every day because of her.

---

[2] Tolkien, J.R.R. (1967). Leaf by Niggle. In *The Tolkien Reader* (pp.100-120). New York: Ballantine. (Original work published 1947)

Chapter 25

The Curve and the Cliff

One night a few months ago, I learned that a woman I met recently had decided to place her husband in a memory care unit. His dementia has progressed to the point that her attempts to care for him at home have left her exhausted, frustrated and weary, stressed to the point that she's seeing a therapist, and is on the edge of developing an ulcer. And she's angry, she said. She's angry that this is happening.

Another dear friend is struggling to care for a family member, and had just cleaned up a "bathroom accident." "I don't know how you did this for years. Day after day."

No one is prepared for these things. Even with all the advice in the world, I wasn't. I came to think of these experiences later as being "behind the curve," "not quite able to keep up," as one source has it. Late to respond. Candy and I once laughed uncharitably at a friend who seemed always to be responding to the last conversation, not the present one. "Eight-bit data bus," we laughed, meaning "slow data transfer rate." Well, that turned out to be me.

That phrase, "behind the curve," was the way I saw our lives. I was responding late to the changes in Candy's ability to communicate, to make decisions, to think and plan, and even changes in her physical abilities: movement, toileting, feeding herself. I thought to myself, "Look, if I step in to help her with things, she loses her autonomy. She may lose her ability to do these things herself even more rapidly."

That's a reasonable position, if the "abilities" involved aren't life- or health-threatening, or dangerous, I suppose.

Throughout the eleven years after Candy's diagnosis, I found myself always somewhere behind the curve, late in picking up that she was now unable to do a task she'd always been successful with before. And until very late, I didn't see what the implications might be.

It was only afterwards that I realized that what I thought of abstractly as a "long curve," an arc, was actually showing up as a series of cliffs. You're walking along with a set of expectations, and then suddenly, you're standing on air. Think Wily Coyote. And the cliffs are always sudden, shocking, downward toward decline. And you never see it coming, and it comes unevenly. Intellectually, the curve; experientially, the cliff.

The standard example of this everyone faces with a family member is driving. Somewhere along in 2009, Candy called me at work and said that something was wrong with her car. She said she'd parked it in the garage, and I could look at it when I got home. I asked if she was okay, and she said that she was fine. When I arrived home, I walked around her car and was stunned to find the right rear fender seriously damaged, the right rear door deeply scraped, the right rear wheel actually bent and the tire shredded. Even the glass had been scratched. I sat her down and asked what happened, and she told me how she'd started to spin out when she left our street, had hit something, ended up in the ditch on the opposite side of the street, and driven out. When she got to the stop sign several hundred yards away, she said, the car "didn't feel right," and so she turned around, drove home, parked it in the garage, and called me. She'd spun, broadsided a mailbox, and then driven into and out of a ditch. Thank goodness it was a Subaru Forester; even with a several-thousand-dollar repair bill, I knew she had been safe.

And I let her keep driving, because I didn't know what to do. She seemed capable. This event felt like a huge exception. I believed her.

This illusion lasted for perhaps another year, when she pulled out of a stop light, and then accelerated faster than she should have in the first half mile. A policeman followed her, flashing his lights and siren. Sixty in a forty zone. She didn't stop until, four miles later, two other police cars boxed her in and forced her to slow until she stopped, up against the median strip. She didn't know how to respond to their questions, and so asked them to call me. I took her home, she got a ticket, and lost her license. While she wanted to keep driving, and I went with her to an occupational therapist who worked with her, she couldn't possibly have passed the test for recertification, and in the end, didn't try. I remember sitting with her in the OT's office, with that rush of terror coming over me as I watched her flail with the mechanics of driving. How could I not have seen this?

In both of these events, I was "behind the curve," too slow to realize what was going on. Fortunately, the only losses were financial, and they were small. Her "curve" had suddenly turned into a cliff, and I was honestly bewildered. I'm certain I was in denial at every stage of this process, because I felt unready and was really unprepared right up until things happened. I felt like I could manage routine, right up until I discovered that the routine had evaporated.

Incontinent, and unable to tell me she needed to go to the bathroom? I discovered Depends. Over several weeks, suddenly struggling to walk? I shifted our grocery-shopping-together on Saturday to hit-the-store-at-7-a.m.-and-wake-her-up-at-8. After 45 years of cutting my hair, no longer able to? I made a friend at

Great Clips, a mile away, who cut Candy's hair, too, while I held her hands.

Repeatedly my expectations collided with a much more rigorous reality. In September 2016, old friends came to town and we met at their granddaughter's soccer game, on the campus where I'd worked for years. We walked a quarter-mile from the parking lot. By the time we got there, she was fading fast, and we met our friends and sat her down on the bleachers. She couldn't recover, and Ken and I, with Joyce along, walked her back to the nearest driveway, a hundred yards away, as the game ended. A photo with Ken and Joyce shows them smiling, her with a half-smile, and the two of them holding her steady against the front of their car. She could go no further, and I ran to our car, drove back, eased her into her seat, and took her home. We barely got up the steps in the garage.

I realized only after Candy died why every afternoon, driving home, my anxiety level rose with every mile. I was steeling myself not to be angry, not to be disappointed, and instead preparing to take on whatever was there, doing my best to love her and trying to remember the joys of our life together.

Frankly, I don't know how I did it either. But some things helped, so that I got better at facing the cliffs, and beginning to anticipate them.

I got smarter. I got smarter by talking honestly with the doctors and especially the nurses. The doctors can give you the overview; the nurses give you the truth about what you'll be facing. In particular, I got smarter when I dealt with the hospice nurses in Candy's last year. If I'd really been wiser earlier, I'd have been proactive, and asked my eldercare nursing friends for a sit-down and taken notes. I'm not going to criticize the medical system on this, but if I had my way I'd sit every couple down and tell them exactly what is coming inevitably when you get a diagnosis like this. One of my brothers commented on our family habits of denial: "Of course, being a Sherry, we just power through it, don't we? Until we can't, of course." *I read more.* The worst source of information I had at first was the internet. Almost the best, for several years, was a book on husbands as caregivers that a friend from church handed me. Published by the Iowa Alzheimer's Association, it was already out of print. Targeted at husbands, it was especially helpful with the grittiness of homecare. Writing now years afterwards, I acknowledge that internet resources have exploded, and professionals are now providing much better, targeted assistance.

I simplified. I simplified everything for her, mostly by taking on responsibilities she had carried. Housework. Cleaning. Cooking. Shopping. Laundry. Finances. I automated every routine bill. I checklisted a shopping list on the computer. I checklisted the housecleaning routine.

I lowered my expectations, and established routines. We had always been active together. Now, we shifted from biking to use our health-club membership a lot more. We walked together, holding hands, when the weather was good. As her physical health failed, we changed activities. When I could no longer trust her to find her way around the neighborhood unaided, I walked with her. In the end, I was supporting her as she was increasingly unsteady.

I started paying much more attention to health issues. As she lost the ability to communicate, I tried to make sure she was getting to the doctor more often, or the dentist. The dentists I worked with helped me a lot, shifting to sedate her more as she became agitated. At some point, some procedures became too traumatic to continue: mammograms, Pap tests. Finally, even dentist visits had to stop.

In the end, I retired. I was lucky. The college where I worked offered me an "early out," and so at 64, I could retire, and give Candy full-time care that I couldn't have afforded otherwise. And so I was able to spend almost five full years with her, sometimes able to step down the cliffs together for a softer landing.

In all of this "cliff" stuff, I was often angry at myself, and frustrated that I couldn't do better. But I was grateful, too—so many of the people going through similar struggles with a partner were much older. Wives, in particular, were devastated. Their husbands were physically much larger, and some wives were incapable of dealing with them. I had enough strength—Candy and I were close to the same height, and frequently close to the same weight—that I could manage her movement and transitions. She had no behavioral issues, such as fits of anger; she was never uncontrollable, and we had been together so long I could comfort her.

I'm not surprised when partners, spouses, are angry. No one's prepared for this, and the most generous, humane, even loving among us are going to struggle. We don't know what to do. We long for the best for this person we love, and late at night we are awake, reliving our failures and watching our lives slip away like sand between our fingers. Finding a little grace for ourselves, a little self-forgiveness, is essential.

Chapter 26

Real Time: Facebook—Regret, Remembering

January 27, 2019

A year ago today, Kath Porten, Pastor Toni Schwabe, and I sat at my kitchen table. In the second bedroom, down the hall on the left, Candy lay quiet, her face turned to the window, still, body cooling, soul and spirit freed. We talked quietly through the arrangements—I had already told Emily and Peter, called Candy's brother Dave, told my brothers on the West Coast, and now we sat.

I felt emptied out, and as I wrote then, shattered. I felt at the time like I had failed somehow. I wasn't there for her final breath, that stilling and quieting that is opening the door to eternity. Earlier I had kissed her and told her I loved her, and then set out on a sun-bright, snow-covered day to run errands. Kath had been there, and walked with her right to those moments.

When Kath called me, on the road, I drove home in a daze, already thinking of what had to be done, working at laying a carpet of the mundane over an abyss. And feeling that regret of not being there.

All the weeks before, a year's worth of hospice, and especially the last month, didn't seem to come to my mind. All the intimacies, all the indignities of those months, all that suffering faced with her, skin wounds, changing her briefs, feeding her, cleaning up, trying to keep pain, dehydration, suffering at bay, just seemed a dream. It took me awhile to take that regret out of the house of my heart; it is like giving a past infection room to grow, poisoning every good thing. It is like anchoring your life to a moment of injury, stretching a present joy back to a moment of loss, deforming your soul. And then, back in July I posted about my dream of her, passing without apprehension or alarm into the hands of a physician who quietly, as she disappeared in an instant, folded her clothes and was gone. Right then, regret faded.

The truth is that dementia like this is a one-way trip, gradual or steep. Every day you have with the one you love is itself, unique, irreplaceable. Savor them, both now and in memory, and gather as many as you can against the day. Our denial of time passing and downward change consoles us, but is rebuked at every stage. When I look at pictures of Candy now, it is with affection, and with a sense of sorrow at the loss. Ah, her smile! Ah, her beauty! Oh, what tenderness! I do not look at the pictures I took during the last two years, because I know what came after. But I would not wish her life longer than it was, certainly not for my sake.

Chapter 27

On Doing Your Best, and Guilt

August 2019

One recent afternoon a friend and I were talking. This person's aged mother had returned home to another state after a several-month's visit. She would be well cared for at home, as other family members lived with her. My friend commented about guilt. "I feel like I couldn't meet my mother's needs," my friend said.

I spent a few minutes reviewing aloud all the things my friend had done. My friend still felt guilty, but marginally less so, perhaps.

This is one of the issues I struggled with when I think back on my years with Candy. Perhaps it is just my own psychology, but "caregiver guilt" seems wider-spread than just my friend and me. I can think of specific instances where I feel now that I could have done more—been more thoughtful, planned better, changed things, gotten better advice and put it to use.

Guilt like this is never-ending, and to some degree pointless. We can't change the past. Lewis in *The Great Divorce*, I think, notes that we can change what the past means, by which I think he implies that our understanding of the past can change, and that what we do in the future can change as a result of new understanding. Those are useful insights to remember. A past failure can help you step to a present moment of grace, as in the ability to forgive others because you yourself have failed.

I often felt guilty that I could not anticipate Candy's shifts in ability. Although I would read up about what might be about to happen, I also felt as though if I intervened too early she would lose forever an ability she was holding on to. That meant, of course, that I needed to pay close attention to what she could actually do, and that wasn't always possible. As she lost the ability to communicate because of her aphasia, I was always playing catch up.

My friend's mother, raised in the Depression generation, is introverted and private. That means that in extreme age she doesn't easily communicate her needs or expectations. Because no caregiver, however gifted, is a mind reader, some frustrations are always likely.

If guilt, or regret, has any value at all, it seems to me, it must be in prompting us to do better, to be more sensitive, more alert, more patient. Long after the fact of Candy's death, my sense of past regret *might* be paying off if I care for those whom I love that much more.

There are some monsters who experience no regret, no guilt, and whose treatment of those in their "care" is careless and abusive. They're not the people I'm addressing. But it's true that even those who love deeply can reach a point of "caregiver fatigue," exacerbated by physical weariness, the continuing responsibility of nurturing, cleaning, feeding, in some measure entertaining those whom we imagined would be our lifelong partners, equals, and lovers. You can reach that point. I did. I'm grateful folks came alongside at times to step in with me, and to encourage me.

Chapter 28

Looking Back—Loss and Recovery

February 2020

When I go back and read some of what I've written over the last eight years, it looks like I was often caught up in public life: politics, for instance, or books read and recommended, or public reflections on a Bible study I was doing with our small group from church. Almost a sermon. It might look like I was not thinking about more personal and emotionally laden issues at all. I was looking at moral life and values and God-at-work in the larger world. Little or none of the sermon stuff has found its way into this book.

Publicly, I hardly mentioned my work in a Christian university. It consumed my days until retirement, and often my early mornings. But when I wrote in public, it was emotionally distant, restrained, pragmatic.

Some months ago, Margie pointed out—with a laugh I shared, and so insightful that I am paying attention to it all the time now—how I deflect a conversation away from the painful or intrusive. It's that sudden mental arm-flapping that tells you something's going on there you don't want to face. *I'm a Sherry.*

This is what we do, one of my brothers said. Instead, you need to slow down and walk back and open the door. Maybe even welcome that topic in, sit down, and get to know it.

One of the doors that I kept slamming shut was how these experiences were changing me. The first step in gauging that, everyone will understand, is locating a baseline. Where was I when I started?

When Candy was diagnosed, my approach was, at first, to carry on. Keep going. I was in the middle of piles of work in my academic career, and challenged to help people I respected and admired. Candy and I were 57 years old. Our marriage was cruising along; we were talking a lot, planning for the future, welcoming grandchildren, and Candy was as busy as I was. I believe that I was an actively religious person—weekly church, attending chapel at the university, reading biblical material multiple times a week, though not daily, seeking to put into practice the moral teaching I was finding. I was trying to be thoughtful in prayer, both for personal and family issues and for the larger movements of faith and justice I was seeing around me. We were supporting religious and humanitarian work at home and abroad, contributing financially to organizations that fit our values, engaged with others who were likeminded. I didn't think any of this "protected" us in some sense, as though God's favor or approval depended on these things. Candy's health had for decades limited us or kept us on alert; always, at the back of my mind, I was waiting for "the call" that I'd be needed. But I didn't doubt that God's defining characteristic toward us is love, not condemnation or judgment. And I equally didn't underestimate the presence or power of damage in the world. But none of this touched me at a core level.

The image that springs to mind is Fred Ward's "Remo Williams" running across a lake: speed is everything. If you don't keep moving fast, you'll sink.

Speed won't save you. You can't maintain it. A few weeks after her diagnosis, we were driving away from the house somewhere, and I pulled the car over on a narrow shoulder on a busy roadway because I was overwhelmed. I was sobbing for minutes on end, and Candy sat next to me, astonished, I suspect puzzled, and asked what was going on. "I'm losing you," I could manage between tears. "I'm losing you."

Maybe it's an illusion, but in that moment the world looks dark, and you have the sense that an impersonal universe is planning to strip away from you everything you thought you had. Those moments came back, off and on, for all the years of her illness. Where is your understanding of "meaning," of order, of wholeness, when you're looking at that? Neat, packaged answers from your youth will not do the job.

I have mentioned earlier about how I drove home every afternoon after work, not relaxing in the time available, not "transitioning" from "work stress" to "home and peace." Instead, I found my stomach tight, struggling to step back from whatever I would face at home. I "routinized" things when I got there; a simple supper—Hamburger Helper became a great friend for a while, or quick spaghetti, browning the hamburger and pouring in Prego or whatever—and then a quick change with Candy to walk on the treadmills at LifeTime Fitness, two miles away. Once home, a few minutes quiet and then helping Candy get to bed. I tailored my expectations by cutting them down. You're not disappointed if you set your expectations and hopes low enough. I ignored what all of this was doing to me emotionally. Not relevant or helpful to getting through the days. And what's your hope like when you're making those decisions? Is it smaller and smaller, narrower and narrower?

Yes, I prayed a lot every morning. I prayed she would be healed. I begged (at first) that her abilities would stabilize where she was. I prayed for more time. And then, later on, I was praying I could comfort her and keep her from pain. I prayed for her wounds to heal. I asked for the ability to feed her well, so she wouldn't choke. In the last year of hospice, I stood next to her as she lay on her hospital bed, and prayed for her healing, her comfort, and her sleep. I thanked God for every day with her. And I meant it, though some of those days were exhausting.

And I talked with others about all this "asking God" less and less often.

Margie was right about my abilities to compartmentalize. I put the feelings I had about all this into a box, shut the door, and locked it. Instead, I wrote publicly about other things. Over the months and years, I found myself writing more and more on Facebook, often extended meditations or "thought pieces" about the books of the Bible our small group was reading. I had no one else to share them with. Candy couldn't understand what I was talking about, and later, couldn't talk at all. I'm a teacher, for good or ill; I want to share and get reaction to what I'm thinking about.

Writing like that paid off. It kept me sane, and engaged with my religious tradition, often more deeply than I'd ever been. I found myself doing what some of my favorite writers were doing, looking at big chunks of writing rather than proof-texting a theological point out of one or two statements I was misreading because they were so conclusive, so powerful. I wasn't doing "Bible study" according to someone else's format, as I had for years, but reading and trying to understand the larger issues a writer of the biblical period was trying to deal with. It was easier somehow to take a long view of what was going on in my life because my reading showed innocents suffering, enduring, and affirmed. Some of them died, and some of them were triumphant. I found some of the certainties of faith a lot more complicated, and the easy answers of the 1970s a lot harder to affirm in a narrow-minded way.

Writing like that also cost me. I was cutting the emotional parts of my life off from people who might have helped me—

not just with the daily tasks of life, but who might have brought laughter or relief. Once we established Candy in hospice in early 2017, the "respite" breaks every 90 days or so were an oasis. I always carried her with me emotionally, but I was with others—Grand Marais, Seattle and Portland, Spokane—with friends and family. Otherwise, day by day, most of the week, I was and felt alone, caring for her. I realize now that I had been doing that for years.

I realize now that my "single-handed" response to her illness was damaging me, making me in some measure a "dis-integrated" person. If your feelings are so powerful, so painful, that you cannot endure them, cannot function to carry on when you must carry on, then you shut the door on them. And they leak out, from time to time.

But other writing I did was healing, too. I wrote more descriptive pieces about the world around me, part of re-discovering the beauty of a place and noticing things. In the middle of planning for the day, thinking ahead, writing lists, I found myself listening to my son, Peter, who chided me once with "Be here now, Dad." It may be a Hindu teaching, but it aligns with the need to be present that's inherent in the Christian experience. "Being here now" helped me so I didn't have to wait three months at a time for "respite." Refreshment became a matter of a new insight, or some days, a reflection on the beauty and wholeness around us. Sometimes, a "re-perception" of what we think we've always known spurs us on to reimagine our lives differently. Sometimes, we miss things that might lift our eyes above the sorrows we are carrying, and that might even transform them or put them in perspective.

For a man who's spent years in front of books, behind a desk, or standing at a lectern, I'm deeply entranced by the natural world. As I write this morning, I'm looking over a snow-covered marsh, thin clumps of reed-grass several feet high covering most of it. The snow has flattened everything but the thin grasses and the four lumps—birds' nests, beaver lodges?—scattered across several ponds. Between the grasses are the crossing trails of the coyote family I heard one night a week ago, pups and parents. They hunt rabbits and squirrels in this square mile of marsh, and the homes a-building on the margins seem not to slow them down at all. There is wonder all around. Noticing it saved me from despair some days. Slowing down helped. Speed won't save you.

The "sharply-observed and rendered" language poets try to use doesn't, I think, start with assumptions about the universe. The poets, like Gerard Manley Hopkins, end with God, rather than beginning with Him. When I'd write about a snowfall, or the sunlight in the tops of the trees, I think I tended to stay away from any explicit observations about God.

Maybe because I didn't feel confident that He was all that clear about things.

*****

Some weeks ago three of us from my university met for breakfast. We eat together and talk every few weeks, because we're "age-mates," or close to it, and have worked together and gone to church together for several decades. Each of us has faced or is facing health issues or some serious challenges in our families. One has a young family member whose prospects are dire within the next couple of years—a medical issue for which no one has a fix. Each of us was in tears as our friend spoke about the likelihood of losing this loved one.

Because the issue had come up, we talked about how we deal—intellectually and emotionally—with this issue of suffering. Do we believe that suffering and loss are ultimately God's design—our human work is to hang on, trust and believe that He loves us, even when some say God plunges us into these things? We may work toward justice, and labor toward encouraging others, giving them hope, teaching—and on and on—but we ourselves struggle with doubts, with silence, with loss. Yes, it's the standard "problem of evil." We conventionally state it like this: If God's good, then He apparently can't be all-powerful, because bad things happen. If he's all-powerful, and "meticulously" in charge of everything, then He either can't be what we call "good," or else "good" means something we can't understand. For some who believe God's behind everything, then even pain, trauma, and loss are "for our good." There's a lot of hurt in the world; this perspective tries to make sense of it.

I am not convinced.

*****

A dear friend recently read over the manuscript for this book, and noted gently that nowhere had I mentioned one of our most common experiences in life, disappointment with or anger at God. I had the uncomfortable feeling that she was right, that I've been ducking the issue, and I've been thinking about it since.

Honestly, I haven't seen anything that I remember in Candy's journals—nor can I remember us talking about this—that would say she was angry at God about her situation. It may have been there, so private it was never written. She may have thought it unmentionable. There was sorrow, but not anger. It may be that she took all of that on herself, for instance in her frustration at not being able to discipline her eating or other habits. I know she struggled and regretted not understanding, as language failed her. I know that for myself I experienced frustration with our situation—and sometimes with her and sometimes with myself—but I don't recall being angry with God or the universe. Shake my head, sometimes, but not angry.

I understand anger at the universe, or at God. I think it is our natural and first reaction to losses that seem unpredictable, heartbreaking. If we weren't angry at the universe, shocked, dismayed, we'd have to be heartless. I want to say this as gently as possible, but I burned out my anger with God decades ago. Let me open that compartment a little. When I was twelve, I lost my twin brother and my grandfather within three months of each other. I was responsible for my twin's death, though it was accidental. For almost the next decade, even though I was outwardly conforming—attending church—I carried a deep anger at God, at the level of wordless rage. My twin was the closest person I knew in the world, and we'd done everything together. Gone. Ended. And two months afterward, my grandfather died, a heroic figure in my life. My twin and I had spent four summers together with him, learning how to ride horseback, seeing the United States in his big Chrysler, camping in Yellowstone, seeing the midnight sun in Alaska, swimming off the beach at Mazatlan. So I felt like I started my teens alone, and angry, afraid, and a little contemptuous of what I thought was other people's naivete about the universe. I thought it a hard, bitter place, with few if any comforts.

It is embarrassing to admit how angry at God I was in those days. But it's useful. Just a few months before Candy and I married, I was forced to look at all my past again, and came to understand that the God I was angry at and even despised had experienced the same kind of loss I had in Christ's action to redeem humanity. God had endured the loss of His Son. And over the following months that sort of anger leaked out of my life. At first, I had nothing to fill the hole it had left.

Being angry with God or the universe is our first response, but it paralyzed me. If the universe is implacably opposed to me, or indifferent, I'm doomed. Human effort is all for nothing. Over time, I came to see something else. If we recognize ourselves as participating with God in creating justice and wholeness in the world, in teaching children, in battling evil, in healing the sick, in comforting the dying, we are free men and women allied with the Good. Martin Luther King, Jr., was one of the more recent authors to quote a minister who wrote in 1853 that "The moral arc of the universe is long, but it bends toward justice." I don't think it does it alone. He has invited us to be part of the process.

And so when I asked God for help as we struggled with Candy's dementia, I had the strong feeling that I wasn't asking someone who was indifferent or uncaring or determined to harass or punish me for sins known or unknown.

*****

At the end of all of this—marriage, caregiving, loss—how have I come out?

First, I'll say that it feels like a web of "good"—I won't call it more than that, for now—has been subtly—and sometimes obviously—woven around me. It shows up again and again through the lives of people who supported and helped us. The Good is not absent.

A dear friend whom I'd known as a faculty colleague came weekly for two hours on Tuesday mornings, so I could run errands, go elsewhere to get coffee or read, and get "out from under." Every Tuesday, practically speaking, for well over a year. Every Sunday in church I'd thank her, because she made life more bearable. Sunday mornings, volunteers from our healthcare organization showed up to sit with Candy for 90 minutes so I could join friends at church. Volunteers: no pay. Instead, they brought gifts: a "prayer shawl" to wrap her shoulders, reading to her, singing hymns for her.

Our pastor, a woman close in age to the two of us, a "late entrant" into pastoral ministry, compassionate, thoughtful, who regarded me almost as a peer, talking about theological issues, prayed with us and alone with Candy. She wouldn't regard her ministry of "bringing food" as highly as I did, but she's a Minnesota woman who knows the value of great chicken soup or a pan of lasagna. It lifts your spirits and tells you people love you. Her visits, every couple of weeks or so, were gifts out of a busy day of ministry and family.

When I was getting ready to bring Candy home from transitional care, *a neighbor who's a handyman* helped me put up a ramp in the garage, sturdy enough to wheel her transport chair or wheelchair up and down. Without it, I'd never have managed through hospice at home. Pure neighborliness.

Five compassionate personal assistants over the course of the year, who regarded Candy as a friend and treated her like an older sister. Full of good advice and tips for me, they made her care lighter and taught me a lot. Their very physical ministry—bathing, applying lotion, washing hair, administering salves and bandages—was a training ground for me. They embodied that expression "the corporal [bodily] works of mercy." *Our nurse and social worker,* assigned by our healthcare organization, could not have been better. Available nearly any time, day or night, if we had a question or a concern.

We shared a particular, deeply appreciated bond.

Compassion is more widespread than faith traditions. Our hair stylist at Great Clips, a lovely middle-aged Hmong woman, treated Candy always with dignity and affection, even as I was forced more and more often to hold her hands to calm her. Her own mother was battling Alzheimer's, and she understood.

I think goodness showed up in other ways, too. Some of them might not appear evident to others, yet I see them as providential. Without them, things would have been enormously more difficult. We had moved to our townhome in 2004, empty-nesters. I came to realize in the midst of all of this that we were in exactly the right place: hallways wide enough for a transport chair; two bedrooms close enough on the main floor for me to monitor her in her last year; easy access via a ramp in the garage (essential in winter); a master-bath shower in which I could bathe her easily; an open plan, so our small group from church could gather around the dining room table comfortably on Sunday afternoons and she could be with us in her transport chair; a small "association" in which neighbors knew each other and readily helped one another; the Nature Center nearby where we could walk easily hand in hand as she lost memory; stores a mile away, and yet surrounded by fields, trees, and ponds between us and them. And the best care center imaginable a mile away, and not even built when we moved there.

Some friends have gone bankrupt caring for the medical needs of a spouse in this situation; our healthcare, my work, our savings kept us from that. My "early" retirement from the university meant I could give Candy full-time care when others have seen loved ones in care facilities for years. Although she experienced eleven years of decline, the last three years were the most challenging, and the last year, as she was almost bedfast in our hospice-at-home, the hardest emotionally. But friends have been almost broken by longer declines, more erratic and unmanageable behavior by their loved one. I am grateful that I did not have to endure that.

I believe even my writing became a force for wholeness and healing, exercises which kept mostly private the emotions I had or the bewilderment I felt. Out of them came a deeper appreciation for my religious tradition, and what a maturing, healing life looks like in the midst of suffering

Through all this, I have not abandoned my belief in a God who is good, who loves us beyond what we can know, who is intimately involved with us—not "from a distance," as Bette Midler sings. I do not believe in a being who has our days meticulously planned and orchestrated, either. I don't believe God is the author of Candy's aphasia and death, as some Christians would suggest. We live in a damaged world, and among damaged people, and we ourselves, all of us, participate in injury and injustice, knowingly or not. Our religious tradition tells us we have an Enemy, an Accuser, and I believe it. But we are our own enemies, too. Candy did nothing in her life that ought to have had the consequence of what she endured. Whether the causes were genetic or environmental—her grandmother and mother both experienced cognitive difficulty late in life—I don't attribute these things to God. I think, on the other hand, I've jettisoned a lot of rubbish and popular thinking about the meaning and value of suffering.

I might well have lost her in 1984, when her heart raced out of control for days on end. Instead, with skilled physicians and medication we loved each other another 34 years, and she saw our children married and five grandchildren born. She changed all our lives, and I'm grateful to God for that.

And at the end of this, two years later, I am more whole than I have ever been. I am sitting down in front of those locked doors, opening them up, and taking up the things inside. Some of those things have been sixty years "put away," some much less. The process of healing is underway. Neither loss nor love disappears.

Candy and I had a long run together. We went the distance, and as Peter wrote once, we "showed up for each other, over and over again." Thanks, reader, for accompanying me. I wish you well on your own journey.

Afterword

March 2020

I owe thanks to many people for this book. Dozens encouraged me, former students and colleagues. My family served as the first audience for this book, in pieces I wrote over the years. Peter and Emily went through these challenges along with me, and their children—Eliot, Taylor, Micah, Caleb, Brie—saw their grandmother change over the years. All of us lament Candy's loss, and we each knew her in a different way. Some of the folks who helped us deserve medals and honor: Dr. Nancy Olen, RN, our "every Tuesday" friend, and her husband Dick; Randy and Pam Brown, Kyle and Jenny Sherer, Shawn and Ashlee Murray, David and Joey Best, Bernie Missal, Kathryn and Michael Porten, from our Sunday Bible study; pastor extraordinaire Toni Schwabe, recently widowed with the loss of Dan. Their love and support for Candy and me in her decline were persistent and astonishing. Bob and Marcia, Mike and Anne, Tom and Karla Sherry, my brothers and their loving wives, welcomed, supported, accommodated, and prayed for us, along with giving the practical, hospitable help that makes life possible. Thanks to Marcia Rogers, who asked a hard question.

And finally, a thank you to Margie.

Margie, Marjorie Ann Mathison Hance, who has been instrumental in this healing process, has said yes to my proposal of marriage. We will marry this summer or fall. "You never stop loving the one you lost," she told my friends Bill and Sue. I agree. But there is room in your life to build on the foundation of a first love, and room for deep happiness a second time with no competition from a lost love. And her encouragement to write this book has helped me think better, more honestly, and with deeper awareness of how Candy and I grew together.

About the Author

Richard Sherry is a retired college professor and administrator. Born and raised in Washington, he graduated from Washington State University, and earned graduate degrees in English literature from the University of Illinois. He taught at Asbury College (now Asbury University) in Kentucky and served as a dean and Executive Assistant to the President at Bethel University in Minnesota. He was married to Candice Shearer from 1971 until her death in 2018. They have two children and five grandchildren.

116

Made in the USA
Columbia, SC
09 July 2020